A YANKEE CHRISTMAS

A YANKEE CHRISTMAS

feasts, treats, crafts and traditions of
wintertime new england

Featuring NANTUCKET NOEL

BY SALLY RYDER BRADY

YANKEE BOOKS
Emmaus, Pennsylvania

Printed in the United States of America on acid-free ∞ paper

The Very Best Christmas Tree by Tony King, with wood engravings by Michael McCurdy, is reprinted in its entirety by permission of David R. Godine, Horticultural Hall, 300 Massachusetts Avenue, Boston, MA 02115.

Library of Congress Cataloging-in-Publication Data

Brady, Sally Ryder.
    A Yankee Christmas : featuring Nantucket noel : feasts, treats, crafts, and traditions of wintertime New England / by Sally Ryder Brady.
        p   cm.
    Includes index.
    ISBN 0–89909–358–2 hardcover
    1. Christmas decorations—New England. 2. Handicraft—New England. 3. Christmas cookery. I. Yankee Books. II. Title.
  TT900.C4B68 1992
   745.594'12—dc20   *92—15910*
                                                                  CIP

Distributed in the book trade by St. Martin's Press

2 4 6 8 10 9 7 5 3 1 hardcover

Yankee Christmas Editorial and Design Staff

Editor: Edward Claflin

Executive Editor: Debora Tkac

Art Director: Jane Knutila

Associate Art Director/Book Designer: Debra Sfetsios

Layout Designer: Lisa Gatti

Projects and Recipes Editor: Jean Rogers

Production Editor: Jane Sherman

Copy Editor: Lisa D. Andruscavage

Photo Editor: Stan Green

Project Assistant: Paris Mihely-Muchanic

Projects and Food Photographer: Angelo Caggiano

Illustrator: Susan Rosenberger

Pattern Illustrator: Nancy Lorenz

Front Cover Photographers: Angelo Caggiano (*background*), George Robinson/
f-STOP Pictures, Inc. (*inset*)

Back Cover Photographers: Angelo Caggiano (*background*), Robert Cushman
Hayes (*inset*)

Food Stylist: Mariann Sauvion

Food Prop Stylist: Betty Alfenito

Prop Stylist: Barbara Pietsch

&CONTENTS&

CONTENTS

ACKNOWLEDGMENTS

I would like to thank Cindy Anderson, Cynthia Foster, Mary Hurley and the Bedford Adult Education Program, Kate Kruschwitz, The Crafty Yankee, The Mary Curtis Shop, my husband, Upton Brady, and my sister, Joan R. Wickersham, for their help in directing me to the many people who have contributed to this book.

I also thank the host of contributors themselves, Amy Harrison Casey, Lyn Danforth, Madeleine DiCicco, Sarah Evertson, Lisa Goddard, Anne Haskell, Wendy Kingerly, Kate Kruschwitz, Nina Kruschwitz, Penny Leslie, Robert McGowan, Phil and Peg Read, Franco and Margaret Romagnoli, Joanne Southworth, Elizabeth Timmins, Nancy Walton, Bobbie Ward, Patricia Alward, and my daughter, Sarah Underwood.

Thanks, too, to Scott Barkman, Phyllis Burton, Max Caggiano, C. Daniel Hartenstine, Marc Kauffman, Diana Mizer, and Janet Perini—and to Judy Brown at New England Nurseries for her expertise and materials.

PREFACE

welcome, all

New England carries its own mystique, particularly at Christmas. Villages clustered around white church spires nestle in our folding hills, windows glow in the early twilight, the air is sweet with wood smoke, and the first light snow softens the stone walls that run beside the sugar bush. Along the coast, where seas turn pewter-colored in winter, resorts are battened down and shuttered against howling northeast storms.

Even bustling New England cities—Boston, Portland, Providence, Hartford, Concord, Montpelier—feel old again at Christmastime. Tall, glassy buildings recede when the skies turn gray and snowy. Now it's the small, solid buildings made of warm old bricks and weathered boards that show up best when you walk the original crooked city streets. Granite mills with rows of giant windows come into their own as well, stretching like bulwarks on riverbanks laid winter-bare by leafless trees.

We seasoned New Englanders like to think of ourselves as a hardy and resourceful crew, in tune with our changeable weather and often severe climate. We have been trained by our forefathers to tame stony fields and stormy seas, to make do with what we have on hand, to provide for the long, dark winters.

Proud, independent, self-sufficient—this is how we like to see ourselves, even though visitors sometimes label standoffish what we prize as prudent Yankee reserve. But you will find that there is always a seat next to the stove for a cold and weary traveler, always an extra serving of beans or a cup of chowder. History says Yankees are an ingenious lot, with rockets, roller skates, and clothespins among our inventions, yet we cherish our roots, our families, our traditions—particularly at Christmas.

Not only do we cherish Christmas, but we like to plan for it way ahead. The moment the first seed catalogs sprout in my mailbox in February, I begin to look toward next December. Strawflowers and statice for wreaths, and calendula. Dill, basil, and savory for vinegars. Muddy March is a good time to repair drying racks for herbs and flowers, bleach the beach stones for next year's narcissus bulbs, keep an eye out for plain wicker Easter baskets to fill much later with Christmas treats.

Of course, when December rolls around, no matter how much we've prepared beforehand, there's always last-minute baking and decorating. But we hope there will still be plenty of time to savor the company of friends and families, to renew old friendships with a Christmas letter, to take 2 hours off to skate across the frozen pond or pour boiling maple syrup candy on brand-new snow—and, most of all, time to rock a child to sleep with a Christmas lullaby.

My dream is still to have a perfectly homemade, hand-made Yule. Most people think this takes unusual talent—you must be an extraordinary gardener or cook or needleworker or craftsperson. But I disagree. Time and attention is what it chiefly takes. And spending an hour or two kneading bread or decorating cookies, working a cross-stitch or knitting a sweater, is thinking time. While making these gifts for the people we love, we have a chance to be quiet, an opportunity for reflection. Best of all, this is a time to work together with a partner, a daughter, a neighbor, a child. Sometimes I think the time making the gifts is a gift in itself.

Traditionally, trees weren't set up and decorated until Christmas Eve; the nutmeats and plum pudding waited in the larder until after the Christmas goose was served. Try putting up the tree as close to the 24th as you conveniently can and leaving it up through the traditional 12 days of Christmas, which begin on December 25 and end on Twelfth Night, January 6. During these days when the presents have been delivered, the house sparkles, and the kitchen is full of food, you can sit back and enjoy the fullness of the season.

I used to think that Christmas traditions were sacrosanct and must be exactly kept, year after year. But my children have taught me that this isn't so. Stockings at dawn and Christmas dinner in the middle of the day worked fine with toddlers, but when they became teenagers, we ate roast beef in fancy clothes after the candlelight service on Christmas Eve and slept till noon on Christmas. The true nature of any tradition is its adaptability. Traditions evolve to serve an ever-changing world. So Christmas celebrations are always experimental, and this is part of their magic. Don't hesitate to try new ways, to drop old ones, at least this year. Nothing is static; even memories shift with time. And even in New England.

So unbutton your overcoat, take off your boots, pull that rocker closer to the stove, and I'll pour you some mulled cider, give you a ginger cookie to sample, tell you a Christmas story. And then maybe you'll give me that recipe for pickles and explain one more time how you made that cornhusk doll. Oh, look, it's snowing! Just in time.

Sally Ryder Brady

CHAPTER ONE

HOLIDAY HARVESTS

gifts from the garden

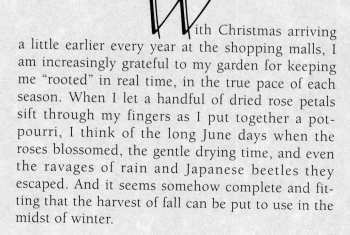

With Christmas arriving a little earlier every year at the shopping malls, I am increasingly grateful to my garden for keeping me "rooted" in real time, in the true pace of each season. When I let a handful of dried rose petals sift through my fingers as I put together a pot-pourri, I think of the long June days when the roses blossomed, the gentle drying time, and even the ravages of rain and Japanese beetles they escaped. And it seems somehow complete and fitting that the harvest of fall can be put to use in the midst of winter.

Why is it, I used to wonder, that while garden triumphs seem like minor miracles, holidays, no matter how successful, invariably carry with them a pucker of disappointment? Now I think I've found at least a partial answer.

While gardeners dream over seed catalogs in much the same way that we all dream over Christmas books, gardeners wisely don't really believe their dreams will come true. The dreams themselves are sufficient—they get us through the dark days of February, the mud and rains of March. If only we could learn to look on our Christmas dreams this way. Relish the dream, cherish the memory, and when November and December roll around, don't try to make it all come true. Every year from December 26 on, I hear people saying, "I'm sure glad Christmas is over!" and I want to tell them "Whoa! Wait a minute, this isn't right! Be a gardener of your holidays—and dream of the next one!"

I think most of us expect too much of ourselves at holiday time, as if all the *doing* will somehow guarantee the dream. No one can do *all* the projects, make *all* the wreaths, bake *all* the cookies they'd like to, every year. But we *can* embellish our dreams and glimpse other peoples' dreams, too, highlighting the Christmas that we hold in our own hearts. Ask yourself what you really want for Christmas. I bet the answer will be simple. And I bet it won't be anything you can buy.

There is a rampant nostalgia for the "old" days, when Christmas meant having a feast instead of a meal, burning a yule log, coming together with family and friends, and casting our cares aside for a day or two. Nowadays it seems as though we add to those cares before Christmas and are too tired, too worried, to enjoy the bright fires, the bountiful meals, and the gathering clan. When you get swept into the swift current of Christmas shopping, maybe it will help to hold some dried rose petals and remember the growing season along with the holidays. And see again that dreams and expectations are separate and distinct. Then when people ask you how your holidays were, I hope you will say "Wonderful!" and sigh.

As for the projects in this chapter, I wish you could see how my living room looks and sniff the heady fragrances that fill the house when I'm in the midst of making wreaths, herbal oils, and potpourris. Some fragrances are as delicate as the drifting traces of rose geranium and crushed lavender. Others are as pervasive and evocative as mulled cider and balsam boughs. Don't forget to pause in the midst of your handiwork, close your eyes, and bask in the perfumes of this holiday's harvests.

MANGER HERBS

Of the five traditional "manger herbs"—basil, bedstraw, pennyroyal, thyme, and rosemary—rosemary is the queen, often covered with tiny, pale blue blossoms at Christmas. Legend has it that rosemary flowers were pure white before the first Christmas. When the holy family took shelter during their flight from Herod into Egypt, Mary threw her blue cloak over a tall group of flowering rosemary bushes. In the morning (so goes the story) the rosemary flowers had taken on the blue of the cloak.

BOUQUET GARNI

Here's a nice gift for cooks at holiday time. To make a bouquet garni that will go with many recipes, mix equal parts sage, thyme, rosemary, bay leaves, kosher salt, and peppercorns. I also like to add winter savory and tarragon. Store in small jars or in muslin bags.

POTPOURRI

An abundance of already-dried blossoms, petals, whole and crushed leaves (above), and oils are available at garden centers and bath and body shops. You can also order them by mail. So making your own potpourri should be easy and quick, whether you have a garden or not.

BASIC ROSE POTPOURRI

There are limitless possibilities for creating your own particular mix, and I urge you to play around with different combinations. I also urge you to stay away from already-perfumed material. It's much more fun to "flavor" it yourself, using pure essential oils with gentle restraint. I think it helps to have a theme—such as woodland, citrus, or summer garden—when you select flowers, spices and fragrances, colors, and shapes. But the following potpourri "base" will get you started.

Materials

¼ cup plus 1 tablespoon ground orrisroot

1½ teaspoons rose oil

1 quart dried rose petals, rosebuds, or both

2 cups assorted dried flowers or leaves

1. In a small plastic bag or nonmetal container with a lid, combine the orrisroot and rose oil, mixing well. Let stand, covered, for 2 to 3 days, shaking occasionally. Then, in a large bowl, mix the oil-and-orrisroot with the rose petals and/or rosebuds. Add the assorted dried flowers or leaves. Put the mixture in plastic bags or nonmetal containers and seal tightly.

2. Place the potpourri in beautiful bowls, baskets, or glass jars with lids (see photo at right). Or crush it finely and use to fill sachets. For Potpourri Ornaments, see page 25.

Variations: For spicy holiday potpourri: Add ½ to 1 teaspoon oil of clove to the orrisroot and reduce the rose oil to ½ teaspoon. Reduce the petal/bud mixture to about a cup and add to it 2 tablespoons each ground cinnamon, cloves, and nutmeg; 3 cinnamon sticks broken into about 2-inch pieces; 2 tablespoons whole cloves, star anise, and all-spice; and a small fistful of tiny pinecones. I also mix in small amounts of some or all of the following: assorted pods, globe amaranth blossoms, cedar curls, oak moss, bay leaves, cedar tips, and strawflowers. (You may think of other good additions!)

For fruity potpourri: Add ½ teaspoon orange oil and ½ teaspoon lemon oil to the orrisroot and reduce the rose oil to ½ teaspoon. Add 1 cup assorted flowers, ½ cup dried lemon peel, and ½ cup dried orange peel. Finally, mix in 1 cup dried, scented geranium leaves and a handful of lemon verbena or lemon balm leaves, if you have them handy.

For a summer garden potpourri: Add ½ teaspoon each lavender, rose, and carnation oil to the orrisroot and mix with 3 cups assorted flower buds and petals. (I sometimes use globe amaranth, statice, lavender, achillea, and gypsophila.) Then add scented geranium leaves or oak moss.

SCENTED BATH AND BODY OILS

At the end of a dark winter day, there is nothing I love more than collapsing into my big claw-footed bathtub filled to the brim with the hottest water. How soothing it is to add fragrant oil, lean against a bath pillow, and settle in with a cup of tea. It's as if some magic softening process takes place, from my winter-dried skin on the outside to my knotted muscles and taut nerves inside.

I don't know how many people like a pleasant bath oil as much as I do, but if you want to compose a custom-scented oil, here are the basics. If you prefer showers to baths, try lightly rubbing on bath oil after you've showered, while the bathroom is still steamy and your skin is still moist. These oils are also perfect for massages. (But try a little bit first: Some people have a skin reaction to oils.)

BASIC BODY OIL

If you use almond oil as an ingredient, be sure to buy cooking almond oil—it's about a quarter the price of cosmetic almond oil. Essential oils come in a profusion of floral and herbal scents and are usually quite expensive for what seems like a very small amount. However, you use only a little, and

AFTER-SHAVE

Men love this and so do I. It wakes you up and makes your skin tingle and your nostrils quiver. But don't drink it! Combine 1 cup 100-proof vodka or ethyl alcohol, 2 teaspoons glycerin, ½ teaspoon basil oil or rosemary oil, ½ teaspoon lavender oil, ½ teaspoon lemon oil, 2 drops of benzoin, and a dash of oil of cloves in a glass bowl. Pour the mixture into a bottle with a tight-fitting lid. Shake before using.

Materials

1 cup almond or baby oil
½ teaspoon essential oil

homemade bath oil, as well as having a purer fragrance, will cost far less than a commercial one. Lavender, orange, lemon, carnation, clove, sage, and rosemary are good oils to start with.

1. Mix the oils together in a glass or plastic bottle and store, corked, until ready to use. (You can get a variety of bottles and corks in many kitchen stores.)

2. To use, pour a good splash of oil—at least a tablespoon—into the tub while the hot water is running. (But be careful getting out of the tub; the oil is slippery.)

Variation: For a welcome gift, make a bottle of fragrant lavender or carnation oil by using lavender or carnation (or clove) as the essential oil and adding a few fresh lavender sprigs or garden pinks (dianthus) to the bottle.

LAVENDER SPLASH

This is a wonderful way for people to end a bath or massage. Mix 1 cup 100-proof vodka or ethyl alcohol with 2 teaspoons lavender oil, 2 teaspoons glycerin, and 2 drops of benzoin in a glass bowl. Pour into a bottle or jar with a tight-fitting lid. Add fresh or dried lavender blossoms. Shake gently after a day or two and before using.

NATURAL WREATHS AND CENTERPIECES

While many people make wreaths with dried material, I also like to start with fresh herbs, making sure to pack the wreath as full as possible to allow for shrinkage as it dries. Most wreath makers recommend using nylon thread instead of wire because it is more flexible and will keep its tight grip on the herbs even as they shrink. If using fresh material, pick your herbs in the late morning after the dew has dried. If you are using flower heads, pick them just before they have fully opened.

Note: Any wreath that is made from dried material should be kept away from direct sunlight, as the dried leaves and flowers will disintegrate if they're hanging in a sunny spot. Also, don't hang a dried wreath on a door, as it's likely to fall apart with the constant movement.

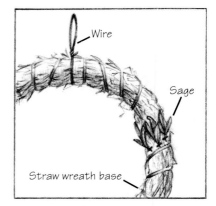

Attach the first row of sage with florist's pins as shown. The next row goes right below so the leaves cover the stems of the first.

SAGE-AND-ROSE WREATH

The sage-and-rose wreath shown on page xvi adds a soft touch of wintriness to the holiday kitchen. The frosty-looking sage provides a cool background to the vivid hues of dried roses. If you grow sage in your own garden, you can pick it fresh and dry it in a dark room: Drying takes about two weeks. Dried sage can also be purchased from wholesalers.

Dried roses are available from florists. Although you can use as many roses as you like, Phyllis Burton (the designer of this wreath) recommends arranging the roses in groups of three for a balanced arrangement that's pleasing to the eye.

Materials
2 bunches of dried sage, enough to cover base
Straw wreath base, 10" or larger
Florist's pins
Glue gun
15 dried roses
Dried baby's-breath
Florist's tape
Florist's wire

1. Separate the bunches of sage and break off long stems. Beginning at any position on the wreath base, attach sage with florist's pins as shown above. Continue adding bunches of sage around the base. Be sure to overlap the stems of the previous row with leaves of the next row to cover the stems as well as the wreath base.

2. When you have covered the entire base, no straw should be showing. Use the glue gun to fill in any bare patches with sage leaves.

3. Glue or pin the dried roses to the straw base in groups of 3, covering the stems with sage leaves. Insert baby's-breath in straw base.

4. Wrap florist's tape around a length of florist's wire. Attach the loop to the top of the wreath in the position shown above.

PENNY'S KITCHEN WREATH

Penny Leslie of Bedford, Massachusetts, arranges silk flowers for major department stores. She also grows her own herbs and rides her bike with baby Annie perched behind her

Materials
7" or 8" wreath ring or coat hanger

down my narrow country road, often stopping along the way to gather wild material for her wreaths.

This is Penny's favorite kitchen wreath. Once you have assembled all the materials, it should take you less than an hour to make the wreath itself.

1. If you do not have a wreath ring, cut a coat hanger with wire cutters, form the hanger into a ring, and tape the ends securely.

2. Make the base by wrapping handfuls of artemisia and thyme around the frame with thread and pulling very tightly as you wrap. Pack the bundles as close together as you can.

3. Gather some herbs into small bundles about 2½ inches long, one variety per bundle. Tightly wrap the stems of each bundle with thread.

4. Set 1 bundle at an angle pointing toward the *inside* of the ring. Wrap thread twice around the ring and the herbs and pull very tightly. Angle the next bundle toward the *outside* of the ring, and again wrap thread tightly twice around herbs and wreath. Working in one direction, continue to add bunches, alternating inside and outside and overlapping the stems of each previous bunch so only the flower heads show. Vary the types of bundles. Make sure that the bundles are packed in as close together as possible. Always pull the thread very tightly.

5. When you have completed the whole ring, wrap the thread around the wreath several times and tie a secure knot.

6. Stand back and check to see if there are any empty spots. If there are, slip in some rose hips or pepperberries, or attach a few strawflowers or globe amaranth blossoms with the glue gun.

7. To hang the wreath, loop the florist's wire in the back.

8. To renew the fragrance, spray your wreath lightly with water.

Variation: To make a garland instead of a wreath, wrap thyme and artemisia around a length of twine or light rope, just as you would wrap a ring. Then add herb bunches, again as for a wreath, overlapping the stems and alternating left and right.

Wire cutters (optional)
Strong tape (optional)
1 big stalk of Sweet Annie (Artemisia annua)
4 handfuls of thyme
Heavy-duty nylon thread
Glue gun (optional)
1½' florist's wire
1 good handful each of 15 or so of the following herbs:

Foliage
Artemisias, bedstraw, burnet (salad), catnip, germander, lamb's-ears, mint, rue, sage, santolinas, scented geraniums (Pelargonium spp.), thyme

Blossoms
Astilbe, baby's-breath (Gypsophila spp.), chamomile, globe amaranth, hydrangea heads, Joe-pye weed, lavender, marguerites, oregano, pennyroyal, sea lavender, statice, strawflowers, tansy, winter savory

Berries
Rose hips or pepperberries

HERB FIRE STICKS

When frost has stripped the basil, savory, and oregano of their leaves, I harvest the bare stalks and tie them in bundles with red or green cord. Tossed on the fire, they give off a delicious fragrance and will also gently flavor anything grilled above them.

LIVING CENTERPIECE

When I went out to the woods to pick the greens for the wreath pictured on the opposite page, every twig, every needle, every pinecone was coated with icy frost and glinted in the rising sun. The witch hazel had blossomed late and the flowers glowed like lucky gold beneath the glaze of ice. Of course, I picked them and wove them into this wreath. I hope you will keep your eyes open for such last-minute additions. And remember, there are as many variations to this as you can invent. The materials listed here are merely a starting point.

Note that there are two "bases" you can use for this wreath. The instructions here are for both a wreath base of floral foam—green, absorbent material that is used by florists in making arrangements—and sphagnum moss on a wire frame. Pre-formed rings of floral foam are usually available around the Christmas season.

Whether the base is sphagnum or foam, make sure to keep it damp and the dish below it filled with fresh water. If you do, your centerpiece should last through the holidays. (Mine lasted well over a month in our chilly New England dining room.)

1. Soak the foam ring until it is thoroughly wet, and insert candles now to make indentations, then remove and mark indentations with toothpicks before decorating. If you are using sphagnum moss, soak the moss in water until it's thoroughly wet. Wring it out and wire it tightly onto the frame in handfuls, leaving the candle holders free.

2. Cut the greens to the desired length (usually about 4 inches) making sure to cut stems on the bias so you have a sharp point to jab into the foam or moss.

3. Lay the wreath on a table or counter and poke in the greens. Working in one direction, cover the inside and then the outside edges (see illustration at right). Fill in the middle.

4. Add the other embellishments. You can jab them directly into the wreath the way you did the greens. Or you can use florist's picks or a glue gun to attach these last bits. Add a ribbon, if desired.

5. Add the candles. Then fill a saucer or plate with water and set the wreath in it.

Variation: For an Advent wreath centerpiece, use 3 purple candles and a single pink one. On the first Sunday of Advent and for the rest of that week, light a purple candle. On the second Sunday, light 2 purple candles, on the third Sunday, light both purple candles and the pink candle, and on the last Sunday light them all.

Materials

Floral foam wreath ring

4 candles

Toothpicks

Sphagnum moss (optional)

Spool of 22-gauge florist's wire (optional)

1' or smaller wire wreath frame with candle holders (optional)

Assorted fresh greens

Fresh herbs (optional)

Pinecones

Dried pods (pomegranate, magnolia, poppy, etc.)

Cinnamon sticks, nutmeg, star anise

Nuts

Globe amaranth or strawflowers

Florist's picks or glue gun (optional)

Ribbon (optional)

Saucer or plate

Insert stems of cut greens in the wreath-shaped foam ring.

FLOWERING BULBS

No matter what waterfront I'm on, from Lake Champlain to Connecticut's Long Island Sound, I look for small stones. They are useful beds for narcissus and other bulbs that you want to grow indoors out of season. I try to get smooth round or oval stones in colors as varied as the shores I find them on; the size doesn't matter too much.

Using the method described below, you can "force" bulbs to bloom early. Bulbs take 3½ to 4½ weeks to bloom. If you start them the week after Thanksgiving, you'll have blooms by Christmas. When I give bulbs as presents, I try to have them in bud but not yet flowering.

CHRISTMAS BLOSSOMS

For Christmas, I like to force either Narcissus tazetta *'Ziva' or 'Galilee', two exceptionally vigorous and heavy-blooming plants from Israel. Make sure the container you choose, whether a pot or bowl, is at least 4 inches deep so the bulb roots can reach down—but it needn't be much deeper than that.*

1. Place the large (2-inch diameter) stones in the bottom of the container to form the first layer. Continue layering the small stones until they are ½ or 1 inch from the top.

2. Place 4 to 8 bulbs in the container (it's all right if the sides of the bulbs touch). Add enough water to wet the bottom of the bulbs. Let the bulbs sprout in a cool, dark place or in dim daylight. Check the water daily; it should just touch the bottom of the bulbs.

3. If you start bulbs in darkness, bring them into daylight when they have sprouted an inch or two. Keep the water level to just below the bulb bottoms. (From the time the bulbs are 4 to 5 inches tall, I add 1 tablespoon of gin to every cup of water. This makes the stems and leaves sturdy.)

Variation: If you run out of pretty containers and handsome stones, you can even use cheap plastic or metal bowls and a bag of store-bought stones you can pick up at the florist or garden shop. Then, put the containers in baskets, with Spanish moss to hide both bowl and stones. Baskets with handles are a help when bulbs get too tall, because it's easy to tie the tall shoots to the handles.

ROSEMARY BASTING BRUSH

To make up a nice basting brush Christmas package, tie three long sprigs of rosemary together with red and gold cord. Give it to the one who roasts the Christmas goose or turkey. You can also tie together a set of wooden spoons and add a tiny jar of dried sage, thyme, and rosemary.

Materials

Stones (assorted sizes), enough to fill container
4" deep container wide enough to hold bulbs
4–8 flower bulbs
Gin (optional)

LITTLE BAGS FOR SACHETS AND HERBAL INFUSIONS

With pinking shears, cut out a calico or muslin circle 7 to 8 inches in diameter. Place a heaping spoonful of mixed herbs in the center of the circle. Draw the edges up and tie into a pouch with gold cord or a narrow ribbon. If the bag will be used for an infusion, attach a long loop of cord or ribbon.

CHAPTER TWO

TREASURES
FROM
WOODLAND, FIELD & SEA

decorative presents and old-fashioned frills

&

There is something ele-
mentally rewarding about gathering what we need
from nature's stores. And once we begin to collect,
we also gain a new awareness of the riches that lie
at our feet. Commonplace, everyday things like
milkweed pods and pinecones, scallop shells and
rose hips, take on a new value when we suddenly
see them as angels or stars or part of a wreath.

When my children were small, they were invet-
erate collectors. No trip to the beach was complete
unless we brought home a slightly smelly bucket of
shells and seaweed in an inch or two of warm seawa-
ter; no walk in the woods failed to yield pocketfuls of

lichen or acorns or emerald moss. I was often eager to surreptitiously get rid of all this messy stuff, but I also stood in awe of the children's recognition of the real value of what they'd found, and gradually I became an even more zealous collector than they.

You can always find a use for these beautiful, free gifts. The ornaments on the tree on page 23 are simple to make and you'll find that new ideas will come to you as you go along, depending on what you have to work with. (Someday I'd like to decorate a tree using only walnuts—or milkweed pods!)

People often think that using natural materials like these is fine for a homey, country look but not so suitable for an elegant townhouse or sleek, contemporary quarters. I disagree. With a little imagination, you can produce something quite sophisticated from humble pinecones, like the topiary on the opposite page. By gilding a perfect scallop shell or feathering a blown egg, you can create a gem that can't be matched by anything measured in karats.

In the middle of the pre-Christmas hullabaloo, sometimes the only peaceful escape for me is to take a walk. Swinging along in the sharp air, I almost pass by the hemlock boughs that droop lower than my head, laden with tiny cones. But I can't resist! Out come my clippers (I practically never go out without them in my pocket), and when I get home, I see that the bucket of water in the shed is, after less than a week, nearly filled with greens. I collect things bit by bit, instead of trying to get everything all at once. That way, the gathering itself is never a chore—it's just part of a walk, a day at the beach, a hike in the woods.

I like to make ornaments with a friend—and sometimes two or three. We try to pick a cold, dark day, perfect for warm kitchens and chatter. I cover the kitchen table and counters with newspaper, set out all the things I've collected, and bring out my scissors, glue, and glue gun. My friends bring along whatever trimmings and decorations they have, and we begin. Cider simmers on the back burner of the stove, spices mixing with the smell of hot wax and evergreens. We help ourselves to cookies, nibble bits of the gingerbread boys that broke coming out of the pans, and work away, telling each other our secrets, solving problems, admiring our handiwork, and soaking up the day.

PINECONE SPECIALS

I had never thought about making Christmas decorations out of pinecones until we moved to a house tucked beneath a great white pine. The first year, I found we were knee-deep in a carpet of big, perfect pinecones that made mowing the lawn impossible. So I picked them up, filling five bushel baskets. It's amazing how many uses I soon discovered.

THE BEST CHRISTMAS TREES

I asked several local Christmas tree growers which trees they favored and what buyers should look for. Everyone's favorite was the Fraser fir, for its superior needle retention and delicious fragrance. Next came its cousin, the Douglas fir, followed by the Balsam fir. Spruces tend to drop their needles more easily than firs and do not smell as strong. Pines have better needle retention but a fainter smell; they are often difficult to decorate because they are bushy.

Choose a tree with good green (never yellowish) color, a trunk that's sticky with sap, and flexible branches and needles. It's normal for a few needles to drop off a tree, even if it's newly cut, but there shouldn't be a blizzard of needles. Make a fresh cut off the bottom of the tree when you put it in water. Monitor the water level in the stand closely.

For a thrifty tonic that will help the tree retain its needles longer, mix 1 gallon water, 2 cups light corn syrup, and ¼ cup household bleach. Sparingly add the tonic to the stand, allowing room for trunk displacement. (Tree tonic is sticky, so you don't want to spill it.) Set the extra aside to add as the first dose of water-and-tonic evaporates.

PINECONE WREATH

This wreath (shown on page 16) looks best if you use pinecones of various sizes. After I've collected a basketful of cones, I usually separate them into four groups—6-inch, 4-inch, 3-inch, and rosette cones (smallest of all). If you've missed the pinecone-gathering season, you can usually find pinecones of various sizes in garden centers.

1. Soak the 5- to 6-inch pinecones and the 4-inch pinecones in warm water for a few hours.

2. Insert the 5- to 6-inch pinecones around the outside of the wreath frame, keeping them close together. Insert the 4-inch cones around the inside of the frame. Let the wreath stand in a warm room for a day or two, while the pinecones open up and become tightly fixed in place.

3. With a glue gun, fill in the middle strip of the wreath with a sequence of 3 cones—a 3-inch cone on its side, a rosette cone, and another 3-inch cone on its side, as shown at right. Repeat with sets of this arrangement until you have completed the wreath.

4. Glue on the tiny pinecones wherever you need to add more fullness.

5. Attach the Ming moss and milkweed pods with a glue gun. The moss gives the wreath a nice touch of "Nantucket gray," while the pods add more depth to its appearance.

6. Attach some cinnamon sticks and cloves to add aroma.

7. Add a bow if you want.

Materials

About 50 5"–6" pinecones
About 34 4" pinecones
1½' triple wire wreath frame
Glue gun
About 24 3" pinecones
About 12 fat rosette cones
Tiny pinecones
Ming moss
Milkweed pods
Cinnamon sticks
Cloves
Bow (optional)

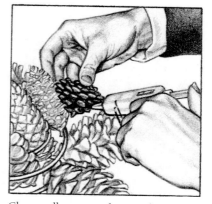

Glue small cones to the wire frame and to the larger cones with the glue gun.

PINECONE TOPIARY

This handsome topiary (shown on page 12) will last for years to come and makes an excellent gift or a stately addition to your own mantel. You can make this tree as simple or elaborate as you want, and if you have room, make a pair!

1. Cover the drain hole in the bottom of the flowerpot with the foil.

2. Crumple the newspaper and place about ½ inch of the crumpled paper inside the bottom of the flowerpot.

3. Mix plaster of paris, following the directions on the package. Fill the flowerpot with plaster to within 1 inch of the upper edge, and immediately plant the dowel or branch upright in the plaster. (Plaster of paris hardens quickly, so don't delay.) After the plaster sets, you can mix and add more to "round out" the base of the tree.

4. If desired, paint the dowel or branch and pinecones very lightly (see "Spray Paint Cautions" on page 106).

Materials

6" diameter clay flowerpot (about 4½" high)
2" square of aluminum foil
1 sheet of newspaper
Plaster of paris
¾" × 12" wooden dowel or straight, thin tree branch
Gold spray paint (optional)
20–30 rosette pinecones
4" diameter foam ball
Glue gun or white household glue

(continued)

5. When the paint is dry, push the dowel or branch 2 inches into the foam ball.

6. Glue moss to the ball. (If using a glue gun, apply glue to moss, not to the ball: The glue might cause the ball to melt.)

7. Cover the ball with rosette cones, using florist's picks or wire.

8. Add shiny balls and small pinecones if you want.

9. Glue moss to cover the plaster at the base of the "trunk."

10. Add a bow to the upper part of the trunk if you want.

Enough sheet moss to cover ball and top of pot
Florist's picks or about 3 yards thin florist's wire
Small shiny balls and tiny pinecones (optional)
Gold ribbon (optional)

Pinecone wreath

SEASHELL DECORATIONS

The Atlantic surf and tides never fail to yield a bounty of seashells. I've discovered that late fall and winter, when the wind-blown beaches are deserted, are the best seasons to collect them. But if you've been a summer visitor to any beachside resort, you probably came home with your favorites. Here are some projects that will show off the best shells in your collection.

SEASHORE WREATH

When you look at this wreath, it is easy to see why Indians used shells as wampum. Instinctively, we want to collect shells whenever we discover them waiting on the sand. These directions are for a wreath that mingles seashells with other natural materials, including moss, sea lavender, and rosebuds.

1. Pull the sheet moss apart and glue it onto the frame, covering the top and sides.

2. Glue shells on the moss, beginning with the largest and filling in with smaller and smaller ones.

3. Poke or glue sprigs of sea lavender behind the shells on the inner and outer edges of the wreath.

4. If you want to add a little color, glue on rosebuds, rose hips, and pepperberries.

Materials

Small bag of sheet moss
Glue gun
7" vine, straw, or Styrofoam frame
About 50 shells (½"–2" diameter)
Sea lavender
Rosebuds, rose hips, and pepperberries (optional)

SCALLOP SHELL LIGHTS

I first saw these glowing lights in Nantucket, where my friend Lyn Danforth decorates her old Nantucket staircase by nestling them among garlands of boxwood cut from her garden and wound around her banister. You can get shells from many craft suppliers or visit Nantucket in the fall and ask the local fish market for discards. Very simple but somewhat time-consuming, this is a perfect project to do while watching TV.

1. Apply a heavy dollop of glue all around the edges of a shell.

2. Fit the first light inside the shell.

3. While the glue is still soft, place another shell on top and pinch them together as shown at right. Work your way from one end of the strand to the other. And that's it!

4. To replace a bulb, wrap foil around the shells that enclose it. Gently hold a medium-hot iron on the edges on both sides until the glue has melted, so you can open the shells and put in a new bulb. Then glue the shells back together again.

Materials

Glue gun
100 scallop shells, all about the same size
1 strand of 50 miniature white lights

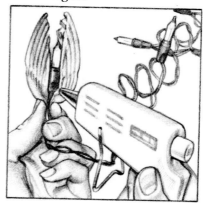

Scallop shell lights

SHELL BOXES

Any kind of country-looking basket with a lid can be adorned with a decorative finial of seashells. This is a project that takes only a few minutes. You can use a variety of baskets and shell arrangements.

1. Before you glue anything in place, try out an arrangement of seashells on the lid of a box. Set them in place so the shells not only look pleasing but also function comfortably as a handle. (A triangle shape fits well into the hand.)

2. When you have an arrangement you like, glue the shells on one at a time, using a small amount of glue.

3. Let the glue dry, then try out the handle. If any shells are loose, reglue them and allow to dry before using.

Materials

Seashells
Old wooden boxes or woven-straw baskets with lids
White household glue or glue gun

SEASHELL ORNAMENTS

Not only shells but also starfish, sand dollars, sea urchins, beach glass, and even some broken shells can be gilded or partially gilded and hung on your tree.

1. If you plan to paint the starfish and sand dollars, spray them with acrylic (in a well-ventilated room) to help hold the gold longer.

2. If desired, paint some or all of the sea treasures and add clusters of berries, dried flowers, and/or tiny shells to the surfaces of the sand dollars or to the inside of larger shells.

3. Glue a loop of thread on each ornament and allow to dry before hanging.

Materials

Acrylic sealer (optional)
Shells, starfish, sand dollars, or other beach treasures
Gold paint (optional)
Berries, dried flowers, and/or tiny shells
Glue gun
Gold thread

ORNAMENTS THAT COME NATURALLY

These unusual decorations are easy for all ages to make, and the materials are free for the gathering. I have found that children are the best gatherers: To them, milkweed becomes a jewel, the perfect leaf, a treasure. Have you ever known a child to leave the beach with an empty pail? So invite a small, agile, bright-eyed friend to scamper beside you, breathless with discovery, while you fill your basket and join in the wonder.

MILKWEED POD ANGEL

Who would have thought that an angel could spring from a field of milkweed? Every fall, before the first snowfall, I try to collect at least four dozen pods to make these angels at my leisure.

1. Spray the pods, acorn or hazelnut, and pinecone with gold paint (see "Spray Paint Cautions" on page 106).

2. Glue the acorn or nut to the top of the pinecone.

3. Glue pod wings to the pinecone.

4. Loop the thread or cord and glue it to the back of the pinecone for hanging.

Materials

Gold spray paint
2 milkweed pod halves (without fluff)
1 complete acorn (with cap) or hazelnut
1 pinecone
Glue gun
6"–8" gold thread or thin gold cord

TEASEL CREATURES

This is your opportunity to create a whole variety of little creatures, animals, and figures to hang on your Christmas tree, using the basic materials listed here.

1. Select the materials for each creature and assemble with a small amount of glue. An acorn, with or without the cap, can be the head of a creature. Use the twigs or grapevine curlicues to make spiral-shaped arms and legs, and seashells for angels' wings.

2. Attach a loop of thread and lift the creature. Adjust the thread so the creature will be upright when it's hung from the tree.

3. Allow the glue to dry. Then spray or brush on gold paint to cover the creature (see "Spray Paint Cautions" on page 106).

Materials

Teasel, acorns, seashells (look for various hinged bivalves), grapevine curlicues, grasses, and/or twigs
White household glue, rubber cement, or glue gun
Gold thread
Gold paint

GILDED WALNUTS

We have two kinds of gold walnuts hanging on our tree. One is just a normal, unopened walnut painted gold with a gold thread loop. The other kind looks exactly the same, but it has been very carefully opened so that both halves of the shell

Materials

Gold paint
Walnuts

Top row: Gilded Leaf and Feathered Egg (page 24), Seashell Ornament (page 19), and Milkweed Pod Angel (opposite page). *Also shown:* Gilded Walnut (opposite page) and other seashell ornaments.

remain intact. We then remove the nutmeat and put a tiny charm or secret message or fortune in its place. (Sometimes people put in carefully folded-up dollar bills.) We then glue the walnut back together, paint it, and hang it on the tree. The challenge for children (and curious adults, too): Find the walnuts with charms inside.

1. Paint some of the walnuts gold, glue on a loop of thread, and hang them on the tree.

2. Open the rest of the walnuts, using the nutcracker carefully so you don't damage them (with practice, it *can* be done!), and remove the nutmeats.

3. Paint the inside and outside of the shell gold.

4. Place a charm or message inside.

5. Glue both halves together.

6. Glue on loops of thread and hang the walnuts on the tree. (You may want to identify the "charmed" ones with an extra knot in the thread, so *you* know which are which.)

BOXWOOD KISSING BALL

Delicate boxwood is among the loveliest of all greens when it is fresh and glossy. Unfortunately, it seems to dry out much more quickly than any other green. Since my husband, Upton, and I like to leave our Christmas decorations up until Twelfth Night, I keep looking for ways to extend the life of my kissing ball. Frequent misting definitely helps. To make a base for the kissing ball, I use a square of floral foam that has been soaked in warm water and surrounded by chicken wire. As long as the foam is wet, my boxwood thrives through day twelve...and sometimes beyond. I recommend hanging the ball up when you are making it—it's much easier than holding it.

1. Cut the boxwood into 4-inch lengths (approximately) and soak the cut ends in warm water and Floralife until you're ready to use them.

2. Insert the wire through the center of the foam and twist a small knot into one end of the wire and a loop on the other.

Glue gun or white household glue

Gold thread

Nutcracker

Nutpick or small sharp knife

Small charms and/or paper strips for messages

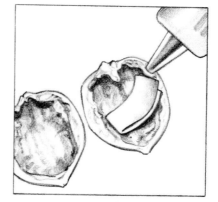

Place a charm or message inside the gilded walnut before gluing it shut.

Materials

2 or 3 big bunches of boxwood

Floralife

About 20" 22-gauge wire

3"–4" square of floral foam

Chicken wire, enough to cover the foam

Narrow ribbon (1' for each small bow, about 1 yard for hanging)

Florist's picks

Wide ribbon (5')

Mistletoe (optional)

3. Soak the foam for a few minutes in warm water and cover it with chicken wire.

4. You may decorate the stems with small bows wired to florist's picks now or when the ball is complete.

5. Poke the stems into the foam. Begin by inserting 1 stem at the center of the top, 1 at the center of the bottom, and 4 evenly spaced around the middle. These are your guides. Beginning at the bottom, poke in the remaining boxwood stems, changing their angles as you work your way up. Angle the shoots down at the bottom, straight out at the middle, and straight up at the top. Pack in the boxwood so the ball is nice and full. Mist the ball with water.

6. Wrap wide ribbon around the hanging wire.

7. Finish with a big florist's bow (see "How to Tie a Florist's Bow" on page 133) with streamers at the bottom or the top.

8. You may attach mistletoe to the bottom with a florist's pick. Then, hang the boxwood kissing ball from the ceiling or door frame or in the window.

Insert stems of boxwood into the floral foam.

Boxwood kissing ball

HINTS ON KEEPING BOXWOOD FRESH

To help keep boxwood fresh, my local nursery recommends dipping it in a solution of dormant oil and water. If you are getting boxwood from a nursery, ask if it has already been dipped. If not, you might want to buy a container of dormant oil and follow the instructions on it for coating the leaves with a mild solution. Boxwood also likes to be kept cool, damp, and away from direct sunlight. Mist at least once daily.

GILDED LEAF DECORATIONS

The wonderful thing about these delicate gold creations is that you can make enough to fill a tree in an afternoon. While painting them, you can also use the leaves for making gift wrap (see page 132).

1. Holding a leaf by its stem, lay it flat on the wax paper and paint one side. Turn it over, paint the other side, and set aside to dry. Repeat with each leaf.

2. When all the leaves are dry, loop a length of ribbon or thread and tie it to the stem of each painted leaf. You can hang the leaves on the Christmas tree, use them to decorate wrapped packages.

Materials

Dried leaves with stems intact
Wax paper
Gold paint
Thin gold ribbon or gold thread

FEATHERED EGGS

Of the ornaments listed here, this one takes the most time to make and is a real beauty. It's also a dignified visual joke.

1. To attach a hanger to a blown egg, first tie thread around the middle of one-third of the toothpick and secure it with a drop of glue. Push the toothpick into the hole in the top of the egg. When the stick is inside, hanging by the thread, pull up gently until it's jammed horizontally across the inside of the hole. Voilà—the toothpick piece anchors the thread. Otherwise, simply glue the thread to the top of a plastic or Styrofoam egg.

2. Starting at the bottom of the egg, glue a row of feathers around the egg, keeping the feathers very close together, so the quills don't show.

3. Glue a second row of feathers just above the first, overlapping by half, rather like shingles. Continue in this way up the egg. (If the feathers seem too long, you can always cut some off the tops before gluing.) On the topmost row, the trimmed quills of the feathers should all meet, and none of the egg should be showing. When the egg is "feathered" all the way to the top, you're done.

Materials

Gold thread
One-third of a wooden toothpick (optional)
White household glue or glue gun
Blown egg (a real one), or plastic or Styrofoam egg
1 bag of ½"–1" long feathers

Glue overlapping layers of feathers, working from botom to top so quills are covered.

POTPOURRI ORNAMENTS

Fragrant but fragile, these ornaments can hang in your bedroom or closet after the holidays, and you can make up fresh ones for your tree next year.

1. Insert wire down the center of a ball or egg. Push it all the way through, out the bottom, and twist the end into an anchoring knot. Twist the top of the wire to form a loop. Thread the ribbon (for hanging) through the loop and tie with a knot and bow.

2. Put the potpourri on a big plate or platter.

3. Apply glue in small sections of the ornament with the glue gun and roll the ball in the potpourri until the ornament is completely covered. Repeat for each ornament and hang them to dry.

Materials

Spool of 22-gauge wire
Styrofoam balls or eggs
Ribbon (1')
About 1 cup potpourri (small flowers and petals—no pinecones, cedar curls, or dried apples)
Glue gun

CHAPTER THREE

THE OPULENT OVEN

a cornucopia of christmas baking

At Christmas, I bake for several reasons: to make edible gifts for others, seasonal treats for ourselves, and most especially, to fill the house with wonderful smells. Nothing calls up comfort and cheer like a fragrant kitchen, from the spicy warmth of ginger cookies to the yeasty safety of rising bread. In fact, I often bake bread more for its psychological than its nutritional benefits, especially when company is coming. And here in New England, although we may keep to ourselves for much of the year, at Christmastime, our houses overflow with friends and family.

When I sit down to eat my last turkey sandwich the Sunday after Thanksgiving, I take with me a sharp pencil, a legal pad, and that old red folder marked "Christmas 1975." That was the first year I started keeping a Christmas folder, and the same one is still going, getting better every year as it becomes a real family archive. I can tell at a glance what sizes people were in 1975 and how my children's tastes changed from dollhouse furnishings to real house furnishings, from Big Wheels to big cars. The old baking lists name those who received gifts from my kitchen in years past— babysitters, teachers, school bus drivers, former colleagues, relatives, and friends who have moved or passed on. It's nice to nod to them again each year as I wade through the butter-stained, doodled-on folder.

Finally, having primed the pump, I start this year's baking list, writing down all the people I plan to bake something for and then all the things I plan to bake. Each of these categories changes slightly every year. While I always make Christ Child Braid, Brady Family Ginger Cookies, and Mushroom Meringues, I usually try out one or two new recipes and rotate a couple of old favorites. Then I match the people with the presents, trying to bear in mind those who have asked for the same thing year after year, remembering the Christmas when I gave one neighbor bread instead of the cookies she had counted on.

There are several tricks to holiday baking. One is to start early, with breads and cakes that can be successfully frozen and stored, then thawed out before guests arrive. Another is to select recipes that you can easily double or triple. And I always like baking projects I can work on now and then, in between other things, rather than a massive operation that takes up most of a day. Bread is certainly one of these on-again, off-again affairs, as are Mushroom Meringues and cookies that can be rolled out and cooked in small batches.

Perhaps the most important baking trick of all is this: Be sure to make *too much*. Then, when the cooking is done, and every loaf of bread and basket of cookies and scallop shell of Glacé Nuts is wrapped and tied and lined up on the counter, you will still have some for the people you forgot. You'll also have some for the ones who just pop in, and *lots* for your own pantry shelves.

I associate holiday baking with many helping hands, some of them quite small. There is no gift more basic or more welcome than a gift of food, particularly when you make it with both your hands and your heart. Think of this as you open the oven door and breathe in the smells of a Christmas kitchen.

CHRISTMAS COOKIE TIPS

■ *For easy decorating, paint icing on cookies with children's paintbrushes. Avoid constant brush washing or murky colors by using a separate brush and container for each color, especially if children are helping you. To get really brightly colored icing, buy paste food coloring from a bakers' supplier or your local bakery.*

■ *If you plan to hang your cookies on the tree, you'll need to make holes for the ribbon. The best way to do this is to use a toothpick to poke a hole (about halfway through the cooking time) in the top of each cookie. If you forget, you can usually still make the holes as soon as the cookies come out of the oven. But work fast, making the holes while the cookies are soft.*

■ *When shipping cookies, make sure they are well-padded within a tin canister or a shoe box. For very delicate cookies, wrap each one separately. Place them inside a sturdy box with enough room for additional padding.*

■ *For padding, use crumpled or shredded paper. Or reuse bubble plastic or foam peanuts from other packages. Don't use popcorn, cereal, or other edibles, which may attract insects or generate unpleasant smells.*

C O O K I E S

Early one Christmas Eve, soon after my son had delivered freshly made bread instead of the usual Christmas cookies to my neighbor, she called me in great distress. She was delighted with the bread, but had counted on the cookies to hang on her tree, which was quite bare without them. Luckily, I had more cookies and another son to take them down the road. So, remember— Christmas cookies are for more than eating. A decorative collection of assorted cookies may well end up on the Christmas tree.

B R A D Y F A M I L Y G I N G E R C O O K I E S

These cookies are very thin and tender, yet they stand up surprisingly well to decorating and mailing. If you can resist these tempting cookies, you can keep them year after year as ornaments. But in our house, we usually eat them by Twelfth Night.

2	cups molasses
1½	cups firmly packed brown sugar
½	cup unsalted butter
½	cup shortening
2	teaspoons orange-flower water (optional)
1	tablespoon baking soda
½	cup boiling water
6½	cups plus 2 tablespoons unbleached flour
3	tablespoons ground ginger
2	tablespoons ground cinnamon
1	tablespoon ground cloves
	Plain Icing (page 32)

In a heavy-bottomed 4-quart or larger saucepan, combine the molasses, sugar, butter, and shortening. Stir over medium heat until the sugar is dissolved. Add the orange-flower water, if desired.

Dissolve the baking soda in the water and add to the molasses mixture.

In a large bowl, mix the flour, ginger, cinnamon, and cloves. Add to the mixture in the saucepan, stirring constantly until completely absorbed.

Form the dough into 4 small rectangles, wrap each one tightly in plastic, and let stand *at room temperature* at least overnight, or up to 3 days.

Generously butter cookie sheets or line them with foil and set aside.

Using a lightly floured rolling pin on a floured countertop, roll out 1 rectangle of dough at a time to the thickness of a dime or less; it's essential to make the dough very thin so the cookies will bake properly at low heat. Cut into shapes with cookie cutters. Lift carefully with a floured spatula and gently place on the prepared sheets, leaving ½ inch or so between cookies.

Bake at 275° (do 1 sheet at a time in the middle of the oven) for 10 minutes. Let the cookies cool for a few minutes before carefully removing them to a wire rack.

When completely cool, decorate the cookies with the icing.

Variation: You may also use Royal Icing (page 32) to decorate the cookies.

Makes 4 to 6 dozen, depending on cookie size.

Top left, Brady Family Ginger Cookies (page 29); *top center*, Finger Tips and, *bottom*, Butter Thins (page 34).

PLAIN ICING

This is my standard icing for Brady Family Ginger Cookies (page 29).

1   cup confectioners' sugar
1–2   tablespoons cream
1   teaspoon vanilla
   Food coloring

In a medium bowl, mix the sugar, cream, and vanilla to the consistency of slightly runny pudding. Spoon into as many paper cups as you have colors and add a drop or so of color to each cup. Decorate cookies with icing, using a small, cheap paintbrush with each cup to avoid muddying colors.

Makes about 1 cup.

ROYAL ICING

This is a perfect icing for Butter Thins (page 34).

1   cup confectioners' sugar
1   egg white
½   teaspoon vanilla
   Food coloring

In a medium bowl, beat together the sugar, egg white, and vanilla until smooth. Spoon into as many paper cups as you have colors and add a drop or so of color to each cup. Use to decorate cookies as described in Plain Icing above.

Makes about 1 cup.

MUSHROOM MERINGUES

The wonderful mushroom-shaped meringues (shown on page 26) are both beautiful and delicious. While they do take time to prepare, you have the option of making them in stages and setting them aside between steps. Assembling the mushrooms is fairly simple and can easily be done by a young or inexperienced pair of hands.

4   egg whites, room temperature
½   teaspoon cream of tartar
1   cup plus 2 tablespoons superfine sugar
1   teaspoon vanilla
1   bag (6 ounces) semisweet chocolate chips
   Unsweetened cocoa

Place the egg whites in a large bowl. Beat with an electric mixer until foamy. Add the cream of tartar and beat until soft peaks form; do not overbeat.

Sprinkle on 3 tablespoons of the sugar and beat well. Continue adding 3 tablespoons at a time, beating well after each addition, until half of the sugar (9 tablespoons) has been incorporated. Beat in the vanilla, then continue adding the sugar, beating until it is all dissolved and stiff peaks form when you lift the beaters.

Line 2 or 3 cookie sheets with foil or cooking parchment and set aside.

Fit a large pastry bag with a wide tip. Fill the bag with meringue and squeeze about a dozen plump rounds (the size of medium mushroom caps) onto the cookie sheets. The caps do not have to be the same size or even the same symmetrical shape. To smooth off the mushroom caps, use a table knife that has been dipped in water.

Make an equal number of stems. (The stems are made separately from the caps and attached later.) To make the stems, use the same tip and squeeze out a smaller amount for each. Pull up on the bag as you go. When the stems are ½ to 1 inch long, slice them off with a wet knife.

Repeat with the remaining meringue to make an equal number of caps and stems.

Bake at 200° to 225° for at least 2 hours, until the meringues are dry but no more than very lightly colored, if that. I recommend baking the meringues after dinner for 2 hours, then turning off the oven and letting them dry out there overnight. This works especially well in ovens with a pilot light. (But make sure you leave a note on the oven not to turn it on until the meringues have been removed.)

Let the meringues cool slightly, then remove them from the sheets. Cool the pieces completely before assembling the mushrooms.

Place the chocolate in the top of a double boiler and melt over hot water.

To assemble the mushrooms, put a small spoonful of chocolate on the underside of a mushroom cap and spread it slightly with the tip of a stem (see illustration above). Then push the stem against the center of the cap to secure it. Be careful that the chocolate doesn't drip or smear. (I put the mushrooms, caps down, in an empty egg carton until the chocolate has set. I also remove each carton from the kitchen as soon as it is filled and place it in a cool, dry room so the meringues don't soften from moisture in the kitchen.)

Repeat to use all the pieces. If the chocolate begins to harden while you work, gently reheat it by returning the double boiler to the heat for a few minutes.

After the chocolate on all the mushrooms has completely set, lightly dust the tops of the caps with a bit of cocoa shaken through a sieve.

Note: Meringues hate humidity of any kind, especially that found in refrigerators and steamy kitchens. I don't even try to make them when it rains. Store the finished mushrooms in airtight containers.

Makes 35 to 45.

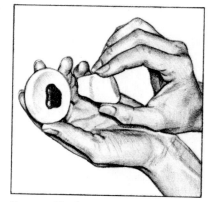

To assemble the stem and cap of the mushroom, use melted chocolate as "glue."

GIFT IDEA

For a double treat, team up a basket of Mushroom Meringues with a jar of Mohawk Marinated Mushrooms (page 61). When you buy fresh mushrooms, buy them by the basket so you will have the ideal container for the meringues.

FINGER TIPS

Like Bourbon Balls (opposite page), these cookies improve with age and ship well. But unlike Bourbon Balls, these are best made in single batches. Children like to shape the fingers and watch while you cut off the tips. And most of them love the appropriate name.

¾	cup unsalted butter, softened
¼	cup sugar
1	cup finely chopped or ground almonds
2	teaspoons vanilla
2	teaspoons cold water
2	cups unbleached flour
¼	teaspoon salt
¼	cup confectioners' sugar

Butter 2 cookie sheets or line them with foil and set aside.

In a medium bowl, cream together the butter and sugar with an electric mixer. Add the almonds and vanilla. Beat in the water, then the flour and salt. Turn out onto a lightly floured surface and knead thoroughly to combine all the ingredients.

Roll into logs the size of your index finger. (My son used to call it a Windex finger.) Cut into 1-inch pieces. Place on the cookie sheets with about 1 inch between the pieces.

Bake at 300° for 30 minutes, or until golden. Transfer to wire racks and let cool.

Place the confectioners' sugar in a sieve and shake over the cookies. Store in an airtight container lined with wax paper.

Makes 2 dozen.

BUTTER THINS

A Rhode Island relative introduced me to these delicate, buttery cookies. The dough keeps well in the refrigerator for several days, rolls out thinly, and bakes fast. While these cookies are baking, watch them like a hawk so they don't brown too much.

1	cup unsalted butter, softened
⅔	cup sugar
1	egg
1½	teaspoons vanilla or 1 teaspoon vanilla plus 1 tablespoon brandy
2½	cups sifted unbleached flour
½	teaspoon salt

Place the butter and sugar in a large bowl. Cream with an electric mixer until fluffy. Beat in the egg and vanilla or vanilla plus brandy. Add the flour and salt. Mix well.

Shape the dough into 2 fat rectangles, wrap each one tightly in plastic, and refrigerate for at least 30 minutes, or up to 3 days.

Generously butter cookie sheets or line them with foil and set aside.

Using a lightly floured rolling pin on a floured countertop, thinly roll out 1 rectangle of dough at a time. Cut into shapes with cookie cutters. Lift carefully with a floured spatula and gently place on the prepared sheets, leaving ½ inch or so between cookies.

Bake at 350° for 8 to 10 minutes, until the edges begin to turn brown. Keep a close watch on the cookies as they bake. Cool for a few minutes, then remove the cookies to a wire rack.

Makes about 4 dozen, depending on cookie size.

BOURBON BALLS

When Upton, my husband, spent Christmas at sea in the Navy, his young sister in Rhode Island sent him a double batch of these quite potent treats. He ate them while standing on the bridge of his aircraft carrier at midnight on Christmas Eve. He says they cheered him in more ways than one. Bourbon Balls "ripen" nicely in an airtight tin and are sturdy shippers. You can easily double the recipe.

1	bag (6 ounces) semisweet chocolate chips
½	cup sugar
3	tablespoons light corn syrup
2	cups plus 2 tablespoons cookie crumbs (use shortbread or sugar cookies or vanilla wafers)
½	cup bourbon
2	tablespoons brandy
2	teaspoons vanilla
1	cup ground walnuts or pecans
	Superfine sugar

In a heavy-bottomed 2-quart saucepan, melt the chocolate, sugar, and corn syrup over medium heat. Stir well until the sugar is dissolved. Add the crumbs, bourbon, brandy, and vanilla. Mix in the walnuts or pecans.

Form the mixture into little balls, smaller than a walnut and bigger than a cherry. Roll in superfine sugar. Let set for a few hours before storing in airtight containers.

Makes about 40.

GINGERBREAD CUT-OUTS FOR CHRISTMAS

One year, we gave our four children two ponies that were delivered during a snowstorm late Christmas Eve. My husband and I had hung the stockings, lighted the Christmas candle, read the Christmas Gospel according to St. Luke, and tucked the children into bed long before I heard the first whinny.

Hoping the children wouldn't waken, I quickly bundled up and went out to meet the new arrivals. The big box stall was ready for the newcomers, with sweet hay and extra oats in the manger, fresh shavings thickly spread on the floor. I crooned to the ponies a little while I wiped the snow off their shaggy backs and suddenly thought of the legend of the talking animals—how, it is said, all dumb beasts are given the gift of speech at midnight on Christmas Eve. I looked at my watch. Only a few minutes to go till midnight.

I'd always wondered what they'd say, these animals, given the chance. Now maybe I'd find out. The ponies nickered softly, their velvet noses nuzzling me; the barn cats, amber-eyed, stared from the loft; the little bantam rooster fluttered his feathers and whispered out a tiny doodle-doo. Suddenly, I felt that I was an intruder, and I left before the first word was uttered. Besides, I had already imagined what these fellows would say.

GINGERBREAD BARN

Although this project takes time, it is by no means difficult. I recommend that you read through the instructions before you begin, so you will have a good idea of the various stages. If you like, the barn scene can become a crèche. Either way, the pattern for the structure is the same. (For the crèche, just use nativity figures instead of farm figures and animals.) You may prefer to use your own cookie cutters in place of my patterns—or in addition to them. The components of the gingerbread barn are gingerbread, sugar cement, straw, and snow. The patterns for cutting and assembling the barn are on pages 38 and 39. You will also need a board or wooden tray, approximately 1' × 1½', on which to place the barn, and some heavy cardboard for the patterns.

⅔	cup butter or margarine, softened
1	box (1 pound) dark brown sugar
2	bottles (12 ounces each) dark molasses
¼	cup cold strong coffee
3	tablespoons brandy or rum (or more coffee)
12	cups unbleached flour
4	teaspoons baking soda
1	tablespoon each ground ginger and cinnamon
2	teaspoons salt
1	teaspoon each ground allspice and cloves
2	cups sugar
	Shredded coconut
2	cups confectioners' sugar

To make the gingerbread dough: Place the butter or margarine in a large bowl. Add 1 cup of the sugar and cream well with an electric mixer. Add the molasses, then the remaining sugar, coffee, and brandy or rum, if desired. Beat well.

Sift the flour, baking soda, ginger, cinnamon, salt, allspice, and cloves into another large bowl. Slowly beat the flour mixture into the

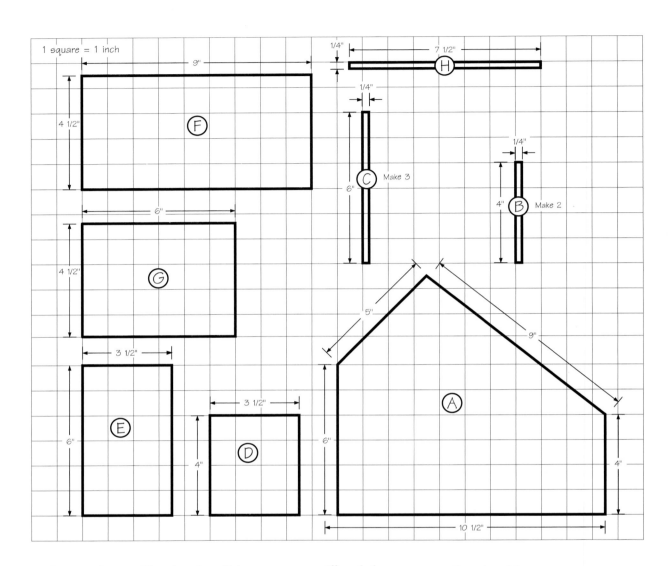

1 square = 1 inch

9"

4 1/2"

F

6"

4 1/2"

G

3 1/2"

E

6"

3 1/2"

D

4"

1/4"

7 1/2"

H

1/4"

C   Make 3

6"

1/4"

4"   B   Make 2

5"

9"

A

6"

4"

10 1/2"

Gingerbread Barn pattern.

molasses mixture. The dough will become very stiff and dry as you incorporate the flour mixture, so finish blending it by hand. Make sure it's thoroughly mixed.

Form the dough into several balls or rough rectangles. Wrap tightly in plastic and refrigerate overnight.

Enlarge and trace the patterns above and transfer them to heavy cardboard. (See "How to Enlarge a Pattern" on page 40.) Cut them out and set aside.

Working on a floured board and using a lightly floured rolling pin, roll the dough to ¼-inch thickness. Use the patterns to cut the dough into shapes, making sure the top side of the cardboard is facing up when you cut around the patterns. The dimensions for each piece appear under the corresponding pattern. For easy reference, the pattern pieces have designated letters, which are used in the assembly instructions.

Set aside the remaining dough for animal cut-outs (see pages 40 and 41).

Take the pole pieces (B and C) and roll them slightly between your hands or on the kitchen counter to round off the edges. You want them to look like poles, not pieces of lumber.

Transfer all the gingerbread pieces to buttered or foil-lined cookie sheets. You may have to even the edges again by gently pushing against the sides with a knife or ruler.

Bake at 350° for 12 to 15 minutes. Don't overbake; the gingerbread should be hard but not burned.

As soon as you remove the gingerbread from the oven—while it is still hot—check the pieces against the patterns. If necessary, trim off any excess bits. Cool the pieces on wire racks.

When they're completely cool, play with the barn pieces so you'll know just how they fit together. Sugar cement hardens quickly, so the pieces need to be all ready to go before you begin making the cement.

To make the sugar cement: In a heavy-bottomed 1-quart saucepan over low heat, melt the sugar, stirring often. Continue to cook and stir until the sugar is a caramel color. This takes 10 minutes or more. Place the saucepan in or over another pot of very hot water to keep the cement warm. This sugar syrup is very hot, so be careful not to get burned when working with it.

To assemble the barn: Use either a small (clean!) paintbrush or a thin spatula to apply the cement to the gingerbread pieces. I tend to paint it on in thick gobs to give a rustic look to the barn.

Cover the bottom edge of the barn back (A) with cement and set it upright on the base board or tray. Hold it still until the cement has hardened and the wall is secure. You will use this same cementing technique throughout.

Next put a single line of cement along the full length and on the bottom end of a 4-inch pole (B). Fasten the pole to the board and the

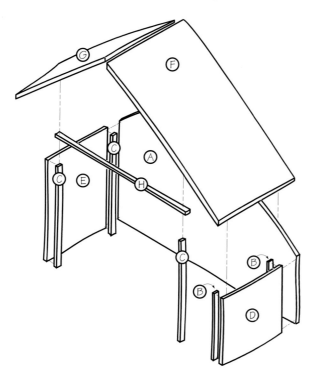

Gingerbread Barn assembly.

right-hand edge of the barn back (A), setting it even with the outside edge of the back. Hold until firm. Repeat on the other side of the back with a 6-inch pole (C), cementing it to the board and the left-hand edge of the back. These poles will help support the roof.

Now put cement on the bottom edge and up one side edge of the right barn side (D). Cement it to the right-hand side of the barn back (A); it will be at a right angle to the back and will cover the pole so you don't see most of it from the outside. Hold until firm. Repeat with the left barn side piece (E), securing it to the left-hand side of the barn back (A).

Cement a 4-inch pole (B) to the front corner of the right-hand barn side (D); position it parallel to the one in the back and place it on the inside front edge of the barn side. This will hold up the front of the roof on that side. Repeat with a 6-inch pole (C) on the left-hand side to hold up that part of the roof.

The roof comes next. If possible, put cement on both sections (F and G) and place both sections on at the same time. This is the most difficult part. On each roof piece, put cement along the long edge that will rest on the barn back and be even with it. Also put cement along one short edge of each roof piece where they will come together in a peak. And put a dab of cement on each outside corner, which will rest on the front poles. Put the 2 roof pieces in place and hold until set. You'll notice that the roof overhangs the left-hand side wall (E) of the barn an inch or so.

You will now have only 2 pieces left, the 7½-inch beam (H) and a 6-inch pole (C). Put cement on both ends of the beam. Position it horizontally from the front 6-inch pole (C) to a place about midway up the long side of the roof (F). (It will be parallel to the ground, as a true beam would be.) Put the remaining 6-inch pole (C) perpendicular to the beam (H), at its right-hand side, to help support both the beam and the long side of the roof (F).

To make the straw: Spread coconut on a foil-covered cookie sheet. Bake at 350° until golden, 5 minutes or so. Scatter the "straw" in the barn (and particularly in the manger, if you have one).

To make the snow: Mix the confectioners' sugar with enough water to make a thick paste. Use a spoon or even a paintbrush to heap the snow on the roof and even on the ground, if you like. If you have trees, put snow on them, too.

To make the animals: Roll out the remaining dough. Enlarge the patterns shown on the opposite page and cut out the animals. (You can also use your own cookie cutters, if desired.) Cut out oval pieces of gingerbread to use as the bases and fasten the figures to their bases with sugar cement. (You can also fasten the pieces to the base board.)

If you have leftover gingerbread, make as many additional animals as you like. I use the leftover dough to make 8-inch gingerbread boys and girls to put in our windows and give to visiting children.

Note: When Christmas is over, place 2 quartered apples on the board with the barn and the figures. Wrap the whole thing—barn, board, and all—in a large plastic bag and twist tightly shut. In 5 days or so, the gingerbread will be soft and delicious. Invite the neighborhood children in for a post-holiday treat.

Makes 1 barn and at least 10 animals.

HOW TO ENLARGE A PATTERN

The patterns in this book have been reduced in size and keyed to a grid. You can easily enlarge the patterns by using a photocopier or referring to the grid.

Using a photocopier: *For a fee, a photocopy service will enlarge the pattern. To double the size of the pattern, for instance, ask for a 200% enlargement. The enlarged pattern can be printed on paper or transparent vellum.*

Using the grid as reference: *First draw a new grid on a sheet of paper. (It's easiest to use graph paper.) Make each square of the grid the size indicated in the directions. For instance, if the directions say, "1 square = 1 inch," draw the horizontal and vertical grid lines 1 inch apart.*

Mark the new grid with reference letters and numbers. Indicate with pencil dots where the lines of the pattern cross the grid marks. Using the dots as reference, carefully redraw the full-size pattern.

Transferring the pattern: *One way is to simply cut out the pattern, then trace around it. With fabric, the easiest way is to use washable "dressmaker's carbon," which works like carbon paper. Pin the pattern to the stretched fabric; slip the "carbon" between paper and fabric. Use a tracing wheel to transfer the outline to the fabric.*

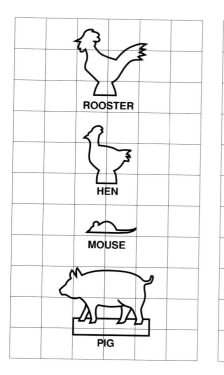

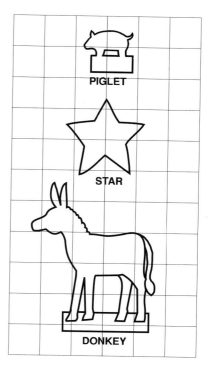

1 square = 1 inch

Gingerbread Barn animal patterns.

SPECIAL CONFECTIONS

There must be a special spot in the heart of every child for candies that are sweet and delicious. I know that I can still remember the first time I tasted each one of these confections.

NUT PATTIES

Our Connecticut great-grandmother discovered this recipe in 1934, listed in a menu offered by A&P supermarkets. She immediately improved upon it and came up with nut patties that were well-nigh perfect.

Butter 24 small (1½") muffin cups.

In a heavy-bottomed 2-quart saucepan, mix the sugar, water, vinegar, and cream of tartar. Bring to a boil over medium-high heat and cook, stirring constantly, until the sugar is dissolved. Cook until the mixture reaches 290° on a candy thermometer (the soft-crack stage). As the mixture boils, occasionally wipe any sugar crystals from around the sides of the pan with a damp cloth wrapped around a fork.

Remove from the heat. Mix in the butter and vanilla, stirring until the butter melts. Stir in the walnuts or pecans. Drop quickly from a spoon into the muffin cups. When the tins are completely cool, turn them upside down and tap gently to remove the patties.

Makes 2 dozen.

2	cups sugar
1	cup water
2	tablespoons cider vinegar
½	teaspoon cream of tartar
2	tablespoons unsalted butter
1½	teaspoons vanilla
1½	cups walnut or pecan halves

GLACÉ NUTS

These nuts look like the handiwork of Jack Frost and are delicious after dinner with Frosted Grapes (page 73) and port. Don't make these if it's humid or rainy—they won't dry properly.

1 cup water
2 cups sugar
Pinch of cream of tartar
3 cups nuts (preferably pecans and walnuts)

In a heavy-bottomed 2-quart saucepan, bring the water to a boil. Remove from the heat and stir in the sugar and cream of tartar. Boil over medium-high heat, without stirring, until the syrup reaches 310° on a candy thermometer (and begins to caramelize). From time to time as the syrup boils, wipe any sugar crystals from the sides of the pan with a wet cloth wrapped around a fork.

Fill a larger pan with cold water. Remove the syrup pan from the heat and place it in the larger pan to instantly stop the boiling. (You could also set the hot pan briefly in snow if there is any.)

Put hot water in another pan. When the syrup has stopped boiling, set the syrup pan in the hot water to keep the glaze runny while you dip the nuts.

Careful cooks pierce each nut with a long pin and dip it separately, coating the nut with glaze. I find that it is much faster and easier to put 6 to 8 nuts in a heavily slotted spoon or a very wide mesh sieve spoon. Don't crowd the nuts in the spoon, and try not to let the nuts

Top, Candied Peel (opposite page) and Nut Patties (page 41); *bottom,* Glacé Nuts and Frosted Grapes (page 73).

touch each other or the coating of sugar will not be complete.

Transfer the dipped nuts to a piece of wax paper or foil. Make sure they're not touching so they don't stick together. Let stand in a cool, dry place overnight. Store in an airtight tin lined with wax paper.

Makes 3 cups.

CANDIED PEEL

There are almost as many methods for making candied peel as there are cookbooks. I like this one, even though it takes a few minutes longer than others, because it produces a very moist and flavorful peel without any bitterness. And the peel keeps extremely well once it's made.

2 **cups packed orange or lemon peel, cut into thin strips (about ⅛"–½" wide)**
1 **cup sugar**
½ **cup water**
   Superfine sugar

Place the peel in a heavy-bottomed 2-quart saucepan. Cover with cold water. Bring slowly to a boil over medium heat. Boil for 12 minutes. Drain, pouring the peel into a strainer. Return the peel to the pan, add fresh water, and repeat the process. Do this a total of 3 times, draining well each time. Leave the peel in the strainer after the final draining.

Place the 1 cup sugar and ½ cup water in the saucepan. Cook over medium heat to dissolve the sugar. Add the peel and boil until the syrup has been absorbed and the peel is translucent.

Lift the peel from the pan with a slotted spoon and place on wax paper, separating the peels and spreading them in a single layer. Let cool a few minutes, then roll the pieces in the superfine sugar (separate the pieces as you work so each is coated). Let dry on wire racks.

Variation: You may also dip 1 end of each peel in melted bittersweet chocolate.

Makes about 2 cups.

FOUR SNOWY-DAY CANDIES

The thermometer hovers somewhere below freezing and snowflakes are drifting lazily past the window: It's time to get out the cider vinegar and maple syrup. Who remembers old-fashioned taffy pulls? Or maple-sugar candy, poured on the snow? Well, it used to happen. In fact, when my children were young, we always celebrated snowy days with some special kind of candy making. I can still taste the melting sweetness whenever I hear the "no school" whistle blow.

OLD-FASHIONED VINEGAR TAFFY

In the days before radio and television, taffy pulls ranked with church suppers and sleigh rides as major social events during cold midwinter evenings. Directions for pulling taffy are found in almost every old New England cookbook and collection of family recipes. This one is my favorite.

2   tablespoons unsalted
    butter
2   cups sugar
½   cup cider vinegar

Butter a large platter and set it aside.

In a heavy-bottomed 2-quart saucepan over low heat, melt the butter. Add the sugar and vinegar; stir until the sugar is dissolved.

Bring to a boil, stirring from time to time (the mixture will bubble up quite a bit, so be careful as you stir). Cook until the mixture reaches 265° on a candy thermometer and is brittle when a small amount is dropped into cold water (the hard-ball stage).

This mixture is very hot, so carefully pour it onto the prepared platter. Work and turn the mixture with a candy scraper or spatula until the candy is barely cool enough to handle. With well-buttered hands, start pulling and folding the mass back and forth, from hand to hand, until the candy loses its stickiness and becomes a glistening ribbon.

At this point, you should begin to twist the taffy ropes while you pull and fold. Do this until the ridges that form during twisting begin to keep their shape. This can take anywhere from 5 to 20 minutes, depending on how many buttered hands you have working the candy and how practiced they are.

This is hard work and is much more easily done with as many strong arms as you can muster. (Growing boys are ideal helpers.) When the candy is opaque, firm, and elastic, shape it into ropes and stretch the pieces out on snow to harden. (If you don't have snow, place the ropes on a buttered platter.) Cut with a well-buttered knife or break apart.

Makes about 12 ounces.

VELVET MOLASSES TAFFY

The pulling method for this is exactly the same as for Old-Fashioned Vinegar Taffy (above), except for the addition of vanilla during the pulling.

1   cup water
3   cups sugar
1   cup molasses
3   tablespoons vinegar
½   teaspoon cream of
    tartar
½   cup unsalted butter,
    melted
¼   teaspoon baking soda
1   teaspoon vanilla

Butter a large platter and set it aside.

In a heavy-bottomed 3-quart saucepan over medium-high heat, bring the water to a boil. Add the sugar, molasses, and vinegar. Bring to a boil again, without stirring. Add the cream of tartar. Boil until the mixture reaches 244° on a candy thermometer (the firm-ball stage). The mixture will bubble up as it cooks, so be careful.

Lower the heat, and stirring constantly from now on, add the butter and baking soda. Keep stirring and boil slowly for a short time until the candy is about 265° (the hard-ball stage).

This mixture is very hot, so very carefully pour it onto the prepared platter. Work and turn the mixture with a candy scraper or spatula until the candy is barely cool enough to handle. Then, with well-buttered hands, start pulling and folding the mass back and forth, from hand to hand, until the candy loses its stickiness and becomes a glistening ribbon. As you work, sprinkle on the vanilla and incorporate it into the taffy.

At this point, you should begin to twist the taffy ropes while you pull and fold them. Do this until the ridges that form during twisting begin to keep their shape. When the candy is satiny, taffy-colored, and beginning to hold its shape, lay ropes of it on clean new snow or a buttered platter until it firms up. Cut it into pieces with a well-buttered knife, or break apart.

Makes about 1½ pounds.

SYRUP AND SNOW

When I look back now on my childhood winters on Cape Cod, they seem pretty nearly perfect. But no matter how near-perfect, it seemed I could never get enough of my two favorite things—snow and maple syrup. Nothing was sweeter than pouring out liquid maple sugar candy onto the pristine snow, where it would harden almost as fast as I poured it!
So now, whenever I am lucky enough to have a good supply of maple syrup and ample snowfall outside the back door, I roll up my sleeves and follow the simple—and sinfully delicious—recipe below.

1   cup maple syrup
1   teaspoon vanilla

In a heavy-bottomed 1-quart saucepan, boil the maple syrup until it reaches 290° on a candy thermometer (the soft-crack stage). Be careful—the mixture is very hot. Remove it from the heat and stir in the vanilla.

Take it outside and pour it on clean, new snow. As soon as it hardens, which takes but a minute, lift it off and eat it. You'll probably want to eat it all right away because it tends to become sticky if it stands too long. But please don't serve this candy to anyone with a mouthful of expensive braces!

Makes about ½ pound.

CREAMY MAPLE WALNUT CANDY

You don't need snow for this one, but like most things, it seems to taste better as the drifts curl around the corners of the house and the flakes hit the windows like fine grains of sand.

2	cups maple syrup
1	cup heavy cream
1	cup chopped walnuts, lightly toasted
2	teaspoons vanilla

Butter an 8" ✕ 8" baking dish and set it aside.

In a heavy-bottomed 2-quart saucepan, mix the maple syrup and cream. Bring to a boil and cook, stirring occasionally, until the mixture reaches 238° on a candy thermometer (the soft-ball stage).

Remove from the heat and beat with a wooden spoon. (Be careful as you stir, as the mixture starts out very hot.) When it has thickened and turned lukewarm, add the walnuts and vanilla. Pour the mixture into the prepared pan.

Let set, then cut into 1-inch squares.

Makes 64.

B READS

For me, the process of making bread is completely different from every other kind of baking and cooking. Perhaps it's because the yeast is actually living matter, and so there are two of us working miracles. There is the swelling, sighing mass of yeast and flour and milk, and there are my own two warm hands. It's a collaboration and one of the best cures I know for the blues or stress or a houseful of wound-up children.

HARVARD APPLE SCROLL

The Harvard here refers not to Harvard University (even though we also call this diploma bread) but to Harvard, Massachusetts, a pretty little village nestled among orchard-studded hills. The reason we call this diploma bread is because of the way in which it is rolled up, like a scroll.

Bread

⅓	cup milk
⅓	cup sugar
3	tablespoons unsalted, softened butter
¾	teaspoon salt
⅓	cup warm water (about 115°)
1	package active dry yeast
2	large eggs
	About 3 cups unbleached flour

Filling

3	tablespoons unsalted butter, melted

To make the bread: In a heavy-bottomed 1-quart saucepan, scald the milk. Stir in the sugar, butter, and salt. Cool to lukewarm.

Place the water in a large bowl and test the yeast as described on page 49.

Add the milk mixture and the eggs. Stir in half of the flour and beat with a wooden spoon until smooth. Add enough of the remaining flour to make a nice, soft, but kneadable, dough.

Turn the dough out onto a lightly floured board or counter and knead until smooth and elastic, about 10 minutes.

Butter a large bowl and put in the dough, turning it to coat all sides. Cover with a damp towel and let rise in a warm place until doubled in bulk, about 1 hour. Punch down and turn out on a lightly floured board.

Divide the dough in half and roll each piece into an 8" × 12" rectangle.

To make the filling: Brush the pieces with about 2 tablespoons of the butter.

In a small bowl, mix the sugar, cinnamon, nutmeg, and cloves. Sprinkle each piece of dough with ⅓ of the mixture. Form each piece into a scroll by tightly rolling up the 8" edges to meet in the center. Make 7 slashes (an inch or so apart) in each half of the scrolls, going about halfway down into the dough.

Butter two 9" × 5" loaf pans. Add the dough, cut sides facing up.

Pare and core the apples. Cut each into 14 slices. Press the slices, thin edges down, into the slashes. Brush the loaves lightly with the remaining tablespoon of butter. Sprinkle the tops with the remaining ⅓ of the spice mixture.

Cover with a damp towel and let rise in a warm place until doubled in bulk, about 1 hour. Bake at 375° for 35 minutes, or until the tops are lightly browned and the sides begin to pull away from the pans. Gently remove it from the pan and place it on a wire rack. You can serve it warm for breakfast or tea. If you want to store the remainder, allow the bread to cool completely before wrapping, storing, or freezing. Reheat before serving.

Makes 2 loaves.

1	cup sugar
2	teaspoons cinnamon
½	teaspoon ground nutmeg
¼	teaspoon ground cloves
2	large tart cooking apples (preferably Rhode Island Greenings or Macouns)

CHRIST CHILD BRAID

This is a versatile bread, with several variations. The filled and iced braid has been the mainstay of our Christmas breakfasts for 30 years. This recipe makes two small braids, but you could make a single large one.

To make the bread: In a 1-quart saucepan over medium heat, scald the milk. Pour the scalded milk into a large bowl. Stir in the butter, sugar, and salt. Let cool to lukewarm.

Bread

½ cup milk
¼ cup unsalted butter
½ cup sugar
2 teaspoons salt
½ cup warm water (about 115°)
2 packages active dry yeast
2 large eggs, lightly beaten
1½ teaspoons ground cardamom
About 5 cups unbleached flour

Filling

2 tablespoons unsalted butter, softened
4–8 ounces thick fruit preserves
2 teaspoons ground cinnamon
½ cup toasted chopped almonds

Glaze

1 egg white
1 teaspoon water

Icing

½ cup confectioners' sugar
½ teaspoon vanilla
Cream
½ cup toasted sliced almonds (optional)

Place the warm water in a small bowl or cup and sprinkle the yeast on top. Stir lightly with a teaspoon and let rest for 5 minutes or so. The mixture should begin to bubble and rise a little. If it doesn't, wait another 5 minutes. If there is no change, try another packet of yeast.

Add the dissolved yeast to the milk mixture. Stir in the eggs, then the cardamom and 2½ cups of the flour. Beat with a wooden spoon until blended.

Gradually add the remaining 2½ cups flour, stirring then kneading until all or most of the flour is incorporated. Turn out on a well-floured board or counter and knead until smooth and elastic. Place in a buttered bowl and turn to coat all sides with the butter.

Cover with a damp dish towel and let rise in a warm place until doubled in bulk, about 1 hour. Punch down the dough and divide it in half. Pull a piece of dough off each half and form each into a smooth ball about 2" in diameter; set these pieces aside. Roll each large piece of dough into a rectangle about 10" × 9".

To make the filling: Spread 1 tablespoon of the butter lengthwise down the middle of each rectangle in a 3" × 10" strip. Then spread the preserves on top of the butter. Sprinkle with the cinnamon, then the nuts.

Crisscross strips of dough over filling to make the braid.

Starting about ½ inch from the filling and working toward the side edge, cut 6 evenly spaced horizontal strips in both sides of each piece of dough. Alternating the left and right strips, fold the dough over the filling to resemble a braid. (Slightly stretch the strips as you wrap them over the filling.) Tuck the loose ends at the bottom under the braids. (See the illustrations at right.)

Butter 2 cookie sheets or line them with foil. Transfer the braids to the sheets. Place 1 of the reserved balls at the top of each braid to look like a baby's head peeking out of the "swaddling clothes." Cover the braids with damp dish towels and let rise in a warm place until doubled in bulk, about 1 hour.

To make the glaze: In a cup, lightly whisk together the egg white and water until frothy. With a pastry brush, paint the top of each braid. Bake at 350° for 30 minutes, or until the braids are golden brown and sound hollow when tapped. Place on wire racks to cool.

To make the icing: In a small bowl, mix the sugar and vanilla. Stir in enough cream to form a pourable icing. Drizzle it over the braids. If desired, sprinkle almonds on top of the icing.

Tuck dough underneath at the end of the braid.

Variation: Instead of filled braids, you can make a large braided loaf with raisins and currants. Add ½ cup golden raisins and ½ cup currants to the basic dough. After the first rising, divide the dough into 3 parts. Roll each into a smooth rope about 1 foot long, tapering the ends slightly. Place the 3 ropes side by side on a lightly floured surface. Starting in the middle, braid the ropes together; tuck the ends under when you finish braiding that half. Repeat for the other half. Place on a buttered or foil-covered cookie sheet, cover, and let rise. Glaze and dust with coarse sugar (also known as sugar crystals or decorating sugar). Increase baking time to 35 minutes and omit the icing.

Makes 2 braids.

CAKES

Dessert lovers tend to fall into two general categories—those who go for chocolate and those who don't. If you want to appeal to both tastes, I recommend the following pair of cakes.

PINECONE CHRISTMAS CAKE

The crowning glory of any holiday dessert table, this is a treat to look at as well as to eat. I'm indebted to Rose Levy Beranbaum for the design of this wonderful chocolate cake.

To make the cake: Place the butter and chocolate in the top of a double boiler. Melt over hot water. Set aside.

Separate the eggs, putting the yolks into 1 large bowl and the whites into another.

Using an electric mixer, beat the yolks slightly, then gradually beat in the sugar. Beat for a minute or so, until the mixture is light and fluffy. Add the melted chocolate mixture and stir well. Beat in the flour and brandy. Set aside.

Using clean beaters, beat the whites until stiff peaks form when you lift the beaters. Thoroughly fold about ¼ of the whites into the chocolate mixture. Then gently fold in the remaining egg whites, being careful not to overmix and deflate them.

Grease two 9" × 13" cake pans. Line the bottoms with cooking parchment. Grease and flour the parchment.

Pour the batter evenly into the pans and spread it with a spatula. Bake at 375° for 20 minutes, or until the cake puffs up and springs back when you gently press it. Let cool for a few minutes on wire racks, then unmold from the pans, peel off the paper, and let the cake cool completely.

Enlarge the pattern on page 52, and cut out 2 pinecone ovals, reserving the scraps (see "How to Enlarge a Pattern" on page 40).

At this point, you may freeze the cake and scraps and complete the project later. I've successfully kept them for 2 months. Let the pieces come to room temperature before continuing.

To make the frosting: Break the chocolate into pieces. Place in a food processor and process until it is chopped very fine. Leave the chocolate in the work bowl.

In a heavy-bottomed 1-quart saucepan over medium-high heat, bring the cream to a boil. With the food processor running, pour the hot cream through the feed tube in a thin, steady stream. Process until smooth (only a few seconds), transfer to a bowl, and cool.

Stir in the nuts and liqueur or cognac. Crumble the cake scraps and add them to the frosting. Spread a generous third of the frosting on 1 cake oval. Place the second oval on top. Spread the remaining frosting on the top and sides, mounding it slightly in the center.

To make the pinecone petals: Before heating the chocolate, prepare the area for petal making by taping a sheet of cooking parchment or wax paper to the counter. Set out a small metal spatula or table knife.

Cake

18	ounces (4½ sticks) unsalted butter
1½	cups (9 ounces) semisweet chocolate chips
10	eggs
2	cups sugar
⅓	cup unbleached flour
¼	cup brandy

Frosting

12	ounces semisweet or bittersweet chocolate
1¾	cups heavy cream
⅔	cup hazelnuts or almonds, toasted and chopped
1½	tablespoons orange liqueur or cognac

Pinecone Petals

8	ounces bittersweet chocolate
	Pine nuts (optional)

Chop the chocolate coarsely and place in the top of a double boiler. Melt over hot water and allow to reach a temperature of 120° on a candy thermometer. Stir vigorously to cool the chocolate slightly. Then keep the chocolate over warm water as you work so it won't cool and thicken too much. If it should get too thick, gently warm it up.

To make the petals, dip the end of the small spatula or table knife into the chocolate. Dab the chocolate onto the paper in a petal shape, pressing down slightly and drawing the spatula toward you, leaving one side of the "petal" somewhat thicker (see illustration at right). The petals should be approximately 1" × ¾". Do not be alarmed if they are not all exactly the same size and shape. The overall effect will still be fine. Keep making petals until you've used up all the chocolate. You'll need *lots,* so be prepared to spend a little time doing this. If you get tired, just set the chocolate aside, reheat it later, and continue.

Make chocolate pinecone petals with a knife or small spatula.

Let the petals harden, then remove them from the paper. If you won't be decorating the cake immediately, store the petals in an air-tight container in the refrigerator or in a cool room.

When decorating the cake, start at the wider base of the oval and work toward the tip. Handle the petals with tweezers, unless you have very chilly and nimble hands. Insert the tapered ends of the petals into the cake. Stagger the rows as you would shingles on a house. If you like, you may place pine nuts under some of the petals.

Stand back and admire your handiwork—and save a piece of the cake for me!

Makes 1 cake; about 14 servings.

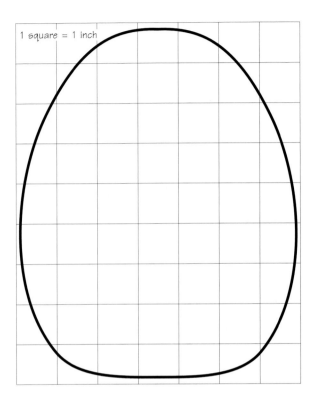

1 square = 1 inch

Pinecone Christmas Cake pattern for base.

TART LEMON LOAF

Citrus is as much a part of the holidays in our house as mistletoe. On Christmas morning, I usually find a juicy orange in the toe of my stocking and we end the day nibbling Candied Peel (page 43) by the Christmas tree. This lemon cake is perfect for eating anytime.

To make the cake: In a large bowl, cream together the butter and sugar with an electric mixer. Beat in the eggs, one at a time, mixing well after each addition.

In a medium bowl, combine the flour, baking powder, and salt. Add the flour mixture to the butter mixture in 3 parts, alternately with thirds of the buttermilk. Beat in the lemon peel and juice.

Butter a 10" or 12" Bundt pan or four 5¾" × 3" loaf pans. Pour in the batter. Bake at 325° for 35 to 45 minutes, or until a toothpick inserted in the center comes out clean and the loaves have pulled away from the sides of the pans. Let cool 10 minutes before turning out on wire racks. Glaze or, if desired, sprinkle with confectioners' sugar.

To make the glaze: In a small bowl, combine all ingredients, stirring until the sugar is dissolved.

With a toothpick, poke several holes in the top of the cake and then brush on the glaze while the cake is still warm.

Makes 1 large or 4 small cakes; about 16 servings.

Cake

1	**cup unsalted butter, softened**
2	**cups sugar**
3	**eggs**
3	**cups unbleached flour**
1	**teaspoon baking powder**
½	**teaspoon salt**
1	**cup buttermilk**
2	**tablespoons grated lemon peel**
2	**tablespoons lemon juice**
	Confectioners' sugar (optional)

Glaze

¾	**cup sugar**
½	**cup cognac**
½	**cup lemon juice**

CHAPTER FOUR

TART TREATS
AND
LOCAL LIBATIONS

zesty morsels for welcome guests

S o much of the holiday food we give and receive is loaded with sugar and butter and heavy cream that I have made an effort over the years to find a few special New England savories that satisfy the tangy side of our palates and sometimes even the leaner lines of our lives. My cardinal rule is that these zesty morsels must bear not even the slightest hint of deprivation. After all, doesn't every diet begin on January 1? And isn't December, of all months, the one for indulgence without guilt? So think of these as elegant and unusual adult treats, delicious and easily consumed.

I love to give people the unexpected—a glass bowl filled with frozen scoops of hot toddy mix, for instance. And I don't mind gifts that are considered a mite unusual. More than one friend has received a sparkling jar of freshly soused shrimp. And once, I sent a soup-loving brother-in-law four large Mason jars, each brimming with a different winter soup. Well I remember the first Christmas after I planted my herb garden, when I couldn't wait to show off that miraculous harvest and give everyone herb jellies, oils and vinegars, and even a few little tubs of herb butters. There is really no end to the gifts you can invent, pairing what's on hand with what people like.

In this same vein, don't forget now and then to do what *you* long to do. For me, it can be just sitting for a few minutes watching the cardinals at the feeder or taking a quiet walk in a light snow. The more we have to do, the more important I think it is to stop and refocus. In our hectic lives, it's hard not to opt for what appears to be the quickest route. I think of all the minutes, the accumulated *hours,* I've spent driving around shopping-mall parking lots before finally finding a space on the outer limits. I dread the long trek past the lines of cars to the crowded mall—and once inside, the dismal feeling of being caught in a commercial web that doesn't have a thing to do with Christmas.

More and more, I find myself relying on odds and ends and supplies I have saved, on the baskets of pinecones and seashells and racks of drying herbs in the barn. More and more, I turn to the pantry and the well-stocked freezer instead of the stores in the mall, as if I lived on an island or a mountaintop instead of the outer outskirts of a major metropolis.

Remember the lines from the Thanksgiving hymn? "All is safely gathered in, ere the winter storms begin." Well, that's how I like to feel when I settle down in my kitchen workshop, far from the bleep of electronic cash registers, the jostling crowds, the bold battery of glitzy lights and sounds. First I have a mug of steaming cider, and then I roll up my sleeves and get right to work.

FLAVORED VINEGARS

Basil, bay leaves, marjoram, oregano, rosemary, sage, tarragon, and thyme are excellent choices for flavoring vinegar and oil. Use them singly or in any combination you like. Sometimes I add a bit of mint to other herbs to liven things up.

To make herb vinegar, take two to four good big sprigs of your favorite cooking herbs and slip them into bottles of high-quality vinegar, such as red wine, white wine, or cider. Let steep in a cool, dark cupboard for at least two weeks before using.

Edible flowers add tremendous visual appeal to herbal vinegars. You can use any herb blossoms (chive flowers are particularly nice) as well as Johnny-jump-ups, violets, roses, or nasturtiums.

F A N C Y   F A R E

When you wish your neighbors an uncommon and delicious Noel with a crock of marinated mushrooms or a little terrine of pâté, be sure to let them know these delicacies should go straight into the refrigerator—the *front* of the refrigerator, where they won't get lost. While some things, like pâté and mushrooms, should keep for a week, other items are more perishable. The Down East Soused Shrimp (page 61), for instance, ought to be eaten within four days. Usually, however, you won't need to prompt the recipients to eat up.

If you want something that will keep longer, try the Vermont Cheddar Tree Crisps (page 60), which will last in a tin for weeks and in the freezer for months.

SHORTCUT HERB JELLY

This is one of my most closely kept secrets, and it's invaluable when I'm pressed for time and merely want to make a few jars of jelly. It's also an easy way to make several different kinds of jelly at once.

In a heavy-bottomed 2-quart saucepan over medium heat, melt the jelly. Stir in the vinegar, then the herbs. Simmer for 5 to 10 minutes. Taste the mixture and add a little sugar, if needed, stirring over low heat until the sugar dissolves.

Sterilize two 8-ounce or four 4-ounce preserves jars—along with lids and seals—by dipping them with tongs in boiling water. Remove and allow to cool. Strain the jelly into the sterilized jars. Add fresh herb sprigs for garnish, if desired. Seal with tight-fitting lids and store in the refrigerator.

Makes 1 pint.

1   jar (16 ounces) apple jelly
2   tablespoons red or white wine vinegar
   Fistful of crushed fresh or dried herbs
   Sugar (optional)
   Sprigs of herbs (optional)

HOLIDAY PÂTÉ WITH ASPIC

This delicate pâté with its whisper of oranges was origi-nally called Venetian Pâté by its creators, well-known New England chefs Franco and Margaret Romagnoli. It is the mainstay of our holiday feasts. Though I have reduced the amount of butter and cream by a quarter, I think the melting texture of the pâté remains unchanged.

To make the pâté: In a large frying pan over medium heat, heat the oil and 3 tablespoons butter until foaming. Add the onions, celery, parsley, and sage; sauté until limp, about 5 minutes. Add the stock, salt, and pepper. Reduce the heat to low and cook for 15 to 20 minutes, or until most of the liquid has been cooked away.

Add the liver and chicken and cook on medium for 6 to 10 minutes, or until the meats are tender. Let cool.

Transfer the mixture to a food processor. Very finely chop with on/off turns. Because of the size of the recipe, you will find it easier to flavor the pâté in batches, so transfer the mixture to a large bowl.

Return ⅓ of the mixture to the food processor. Add ⅓ of the butter, cream, brandy, nutmeg, mustard, and orange peel. Process until smooth, creamy, and perfectly blended. Transfer to a large bowl. Repeat twice to use the remaining ingredients.

Fold olives or truffles into the mixture; cover tightly and chill.

To make the aspic: Assemble a variety of pâté tins that will hold a total of about 8 cups of mixture. Place them in the freezer.

Empty the gelatin packets into a 2-quart saucepan. Stir in ½ cup of the chicken stock and allow the gelatin to soften for about 5 minutes. Stir in the beef stock and the remaining chicken stock. Stir over medium heat until the gelatin has dissolved completely.

Place the pan in the refrigerator until the aspic becomes syrupy.

Brush or spoon thin layers of the aspic on the bottoms and sides of the tins, returning the tins to the freezer between coats. After you have a good base coat on the bottom of the tins, you can add some decorations. Try a sprig of fresh tarragon or dill, or make a fancier garnish with sage leaves, sliced olives or truffles, and bits of red pepper. Secure the decorations with another thin coat or two of aspic.

When the tins are evenly and well coated, carefully fill them with the pâté. Cover with plastic wrap and chill well (do not return the tins to the freezer).

To serve, dip a pan in hot water nearly up to its rim for 2 to 3 minutes. Then turn the pâté out onto a plate or a foil-covered piece of sturdy cardboard. Slice with a sharp knife. Gently but securely wrap leftovers in plastic.

Makes about 8 cups.

Pâté

- 3 tablespoons olive oil
- 3 tablespoons unsalted butter
- 2 onions, thinly sliced
- ½ celery stalk, minced
- 3 rounded tablespoons minced Italian parsley
- 5 sage leaves or 1 teaspoon dried sage
- 1 cup chicken stock
- 1 teaspoon salt
- ½ teaspoon ground pepper
- 2 pounds calf's liver, cubed
- 1 pound boneless skinless chicken breasts, cubed
- 1 pound unsalted butter, softened
- ¾ cup light cream
- 6 tablespoons brandy
- 3 rounded teaspoons ground nutmeg
- 2½ teaspoons Dijon mustard

  Grated peel of ½ large orange
- 8 mammoth black ripe olives or 1 black truffle, chopped

Aspic

- 3 packets unflavored gelatin
- 2 cans (11 ounces each) chicken stock
- 1 can (11 ounces) beef stock

  Sprigs of herbs, sliced black olives or truffles, red pepper pieces

Delicious hors d'oeuvres for the holidays: Down East Soused Shrimp and Mohawk Marinated Mushrooms (page 61), Holiday Pâté with Aspic, and Vermont Cheddar Tree Crisps (page 60).

VERMONT CHEDDAR TREE CRISPS

This recipe came from my favorite neighbor, Madi, who could whip up a batch with one hand while she painted Christmas angels with the other. That was 15 years ago, and while we are now separated by several cities, I can still see her choosing her steps down the snowy path, a hot cookie sheet of tree crisps superbly balanced in one hand, with dogs and children following at her heels.

1	cup unbleached flour
⅓	cup unsalted butter, cut into pieces
¼	cup shredded sharp Cheddar cheese
3	tablespoons grated Parmesan or Romano cheese
1	teaspoon salt
	Pinch of ground red pepper or chili pepper
2–3	tablespoons ice water

Put the flour, butter, Cheddar, Parmesan or Romano, salt, and pepper in the work bowl of a food processor. Process with on/off turns until the mixture is uniformly the texture of coarse meal.

With the machine running, add 1 tablespoon of the ice water at a time through the feed tube, using only enough for the mixture to form loose clumps. Empty the work bowl onto a lightly floured counter and briefly knead the mass into a rectangle. (If you doubled the recipe, form 2 rectangles.)

Wrap the dough tightly in plastic and refrigerate at least overnight.

Butter at least 4 cookie sheets and set aside. Dust the dough with flour and place on a lightly floured surface. Roll out very thinly (the thickness of a dime or less). Cut into small trees or other shapes, such as stars. I use tree-shaped cookie cutters that are about 2¼" × 1½". By rolling the dough really thin, carefully cutting out the trees to minimize waste, and rerolling the scraps, I get quite a few tiny crackers from a batch of dough.

Place the dough on the prepared sheets and bake at 375° for 10 minutes, or until golden and puffy. These are best served piping hot, but no one seems to mind a bit eating them cold.

Makes about 40, depending on size.

PICKLED WALNUT MEATS

You won't find this unusual dish on many tables, although it surely belongs there. Pickled walnuts are superb with goose, duck, pheasant, or even a "lowly" turkey. My first jar accompanied a smoked pheasant, and it was a perfect partnership.

1	pint cider vinegar
1	cup sugar
1	teaspoon ground cinnamon
1	teaspoon ground allspice
2	pounds walnut halves

In a heavy-bottomed 2-quart saucepan over medium heat, bring the vinegar, sugar, cinnamon, and allspice to a boil. Reduce the heat, add the walnuts, and simmer for 15 minutes.

Let cool, pack into sealed containers, and refrigerate for up to a month.

Makes 2 pints.

DOWN EAST SOUSED SHRIMP

You can make this in minutes if you buy fresh shrimp already cooked, shelled, and deveined. I use medium or large shrimp, depending on the fullness of my wallet. I never choose tiny salad shrimp or jumbos, and I never settle for canned or frozen ones. And I always double the recipe—at least.

1½	pounds cooked shrimp
½	cup dry vermouth
2½	tablespoons tarragon vinegar
4	shallots, minced
3	scallions, chopped
2–3	cloves garlic, minced
2	teaspoons chopped fresh tarragon or 1 teaspoon dried
1	teaspoon chopped fresh rosemary or ½ teaspoon dried
1	teaspoon chopped fresh thyme or ⅛ teaspoon dried
½	cup virgin olive oil
1	teaspoon Dijon mustard
¾	teaspoon coarse salt
¾	teaspoon ground black pepper

Shell and devein the shrimp. Loosely fill a beautiful 6-cup jar or crock with the prepared shrimp. Add enough cold water to cover the shrimp. Then, pour the water into a measuring cup to find out how much of the "sousing" liquid you will need. (This recipe makes slightly more than 1 cup, so adjust the quantity if you need to.)

In a 1-quart stainless steel saucepan, combine the vermouth and vinegar. Add the shallots, scallions, garlic, tarragon, rosemary, and thyme. Simmer for a few minutes.

Remove from the heat and whisk in the remaining ingredients. Pour over the shrimp. Cover or seal the containers and store in the refrigerator. You can serve them as soon as they've had a chance to chill a bit—or store them in the sealed containers for up to 4 days.

Makes about 6 cups.

MOHAWK MARINATED MUSHROOMS

This is a wonderful recipe for experimenting. Into the marinade can go whatever herbs, herbal vinegars, and oils you have on hand. The quantities here are quite arbitrary, and you should feel free to adjust them to your own liking. I have chosen dill in this version because it goes nicely with mushrooms and is usually available fresh in December.

1	pound small mushrooms, cleaned and trimmed
6	shallots, coarsely chopped
2	cloves garlic
4	sprigs of dill
3	sprigs of parsley
1	teaspoon salt
1	teaspoon Dijon mustard
	Scant teaspoon sugar
	Ground black pepper
¾	cup virgin olive oil
¼	cup dill vinegar
3	tablespoons red wine vinegar
1	teaspoon dill seeds
1	teaspoon black, white, or green peppercorns
	Sprig of dill

Loosely fill a quart jar with the mushrooms and add enough cold water to cover them. Now pour the water into a measuring cup to find out how much of the marinating liquid you will need. (This recipe makes slightly more than 1 cup, so adjust the quantity if you need to.)

Using a food processor, mince the shallots and garlic with on/off turns. Add the dill and parsley; mince with on/off turns. Add the salt, mustard, sugar, and pepper; mix briefly. With the machine running, pour in the oil and vinegars.

Remove the lid from the work bowl and stir in the dill seeds and peppercorns. Pour the mixture over the mushrooms in the jar. Add a sprig of fresh dill, cover tightly, and refrigerate.

Makes about 1 quart.

BRACING BREWS

Who knows where these Christmas concoctions originate? Some are part of family tradition, others borrowed from the recipe files of friends and neighbors. Whether you choose a toddy or a shrub, be sure to enjoy it correctly: Put your feet up, sip slowly, and relish some leisure along with the libation.

FROZEN HOT TODDY

Nothing warms you up after an afternoon of skiing or skating like a hot toddy (see photo on page 54). I like to keep at least one batch in my freezer, ready to heat up at a moment's notice. The whiskey or rum is optional—the toddy tastes equally delicious with or without it.

1 pound unsalted butter, softened
1 box (1 pound) confectioners' sugar
1 box (1 pound) brown sugar
2 teaspoons ground cinnamon
1 quart vanilla ice cream, softened
Rum or whiskey (optional)
Boiling water
Ground nutmeg

In a large bowl or food processor, thoroughly cream together the butter, confectioners' sugar, brown sugar, and cinnamon. Add the ice cream and quickly blend well. Pack into freezer containers and freeze for up to 3 months.

You have your choice when it comes to actually serving the toddies. If you're making enough for a crowd, you might want to thaw a container's worth of the mixture in the refrigerator (where it will keep for a couple of weeks). Place a tablespoon per serving in each mug. Add 1 ounce of rum or whiskey if you want and fill the mugs with about 6 ounces of boiling water. Sprinkle with nutmeg.

Makes about 50 toddies.

COLONIAL RUM SHRUB

My sister is famous for her rum shrubs. Oh, those long July evenings on Cape Cod, sipping the smoothest concoctions imaginable while sailboats drifted home in the setting sun. But this is by no means just a summer cooler; nothing tastes better after a vigorous skate on the Concord River than a tall, velvety shrub.

1 quart dark rum
1 quart water
3 cups bottled lime juice (such as Rose's)
2 cups superfine sugar
Soda water

In a gallon jar, mix the rum, water, lime juice, and sugar. Let stand at room temperature for 7 days, and it will be ready to serve.

To serve, fill tall glasses with ice. Add the rum mix and soda water to taste (most people like a half-and-half combination).

Makes enough mix for about 16 shrubs.

CRANBERRY PUNCH
WITH CRANBERRY ICE WREATH

You may wonder why anyone would want an icy drink when the weather outside is frosty, but this cranberry punch always tastes just right. The ice wreath and punch are made separately, then combined just before serving. Place the punch bowl in the center of the holiday table and you'll quickly draw a crowd.

To make the ice wreath: Combine the water and cranberry juice in a large bowl.

Place cranberries and mint leaves in the bottom of a 1-quart ring mold. Add just enough of the juice mixture to cover them, and refrigerate the rest of the juice. Freeze the ring until solid; that will anchor the decorations and keep them from floating to the top when you add the remaining juice. Add the remaining juice and freeze until solid.

To make the punch: Combine the water, tea, cranberry juice, and citrus concentrates in a punch bowl that holds at least 2 gallons (3 gallons if you plan to add rum).

Just before serving, stir in the ginger ale and the rum, if desired.

To unmold the ice wreath, dip the mold briefly in hot water. Invert it and ease out the frozen wreath. Float the wreath in the punch and admire your handiwork.

Makes about 1½ gallons of punch.

Ice Wreath

- 2 cups water
- 2 cups cranberry juice
- Cranberries
- Mint leaves

Punch

- 2 quarts water
- 6 cups Earl Grey tea
- 4 cups cranberry juice
- 1 can (12 ounces) frozen orange juice concentrate, thawed
- 1 can (12 ounces) frozen pineapple juice concentrate, thawed
- 1 can (12 ounces) frozen lemonade concentrate, thawed
- 1 quart ginger ale
- 6–7 cups rum (optional)

CHAPTER FIVE

THREE FESTIVE MENUS

delectable meals for joyful times

F easts have always been the heart of all celebrations, happy or solemn, sacred or secular. The world may be shrinking, the universe expanding, yet still we break bread together.

Norman Rockwell, perhaps more than anyone else, has given us the American holiday feast, perfect in its very imperfections. Look into the dining rooms in his pictures of the classic family gathering and you can almost smell the turkey, feel the bustle in the hot kitchen, hear the rising voices of hungry children and the soothing whispers of grandmothers. Most of us, I think, long for just this gathering, just this food—and for this feeling of being connected. But the Norman Rockwell family, like our own, is probably a little unraveled at these reunions. Everyone there probably works too hard, too; tries too hard; competes; squabbles; gets too tired—and, like us, probably holds tight all the rest of the year to that simple feeling of connectedness that one gets crowded around a table with more than enough to eat.

Where most of us run into trouble, and get more overworked than perhaps is necessary, is when the feasts we have in mind are perfect. We worry about ironed napkins, matching glasses, and my particular pitfall, tricky recipes we should have tried out beforehand. When we squeeze in the last chair that really doesn't fit around the table, when we begin to fret about Uncle Will boring Cousin Em to death with his politics, or Gran's reaction to Andrew's shaved head, maybe this is the time to think of Norman Rockwell again...of the perfectly imperfect family feast...of how, deep down, all we really want is the elbow-to-elbow reassurance of repeating tradition.

The Brady Christmases have had several different faces over the 30 years that we've been a family. Even when Upton and I were first living in New York City—days when there were too few dollars and too many diapers—we always made sure we had a real Christmas feast and that we shared it with as many friends and relatives as possible. Our table has always been just a little too small, and I hope it stays that way.

Those first few Christmases, I can remember experimenting with fancy menus that included such foolish challenges as Oysters Rockefeller (forgetting how long it takes to open oysters) and Roast Goose (not knowing how many times I'd have to pour off splattering fat with a baby on my hip). Until at last, I figured out how to prepare a first-class feast and still enjoy the rest of Christmas.

Right now, we're in a child-free interim between children and grandchildren, and our Christmases are unnaturally orderly, almost elegant, an amazing contrast to what they used to be. For the cook, repetition has helped, since Christmas dinner has stayed the same for at least 25 years.

Late in the afternoon on December 24, we'll have a cup of chowder, climb out of our blue jeans and into our velvet skirts and jackets, then set off for a Christmas vigil with candles and crèches and caroling choirboys. When we get home, we light votive candles in every downstairs window and tall candles on the table and the sideboard, their flickering lights reflected and refracted from each polished spoon and fork and tall-stemmed (but possibly unmatched) glass. We nibble on cheese and peppers and open a present or two while we wait for the Yorkshire pudding to puff.

Finally replete, the last chocolate petal of the Pinecone Christmas Cake (see page 50) dissolved on our tongues, we go to bed. We know that younger couples may be struggling through the long night to put together toys whose directions seem deliberately confusing, slapping the final coat of quick-drying enamel on the puppet theater, or finishing the bride doll's trousseau. But we tuck in soundly, free of those responsibilities—and on Christmas morning now, we sleep as late as we want to.

When the children were little, the rule was that no one could get up until Upton and I marched through the house, singing "Hark! the Herald Angels Sing" at the top of our voices. Then the children would line up at the living room door, youngest to oldest, and wait impatiently while we made sure everything was ready, the fire blazing, the stockings all propped up and overflowing, the train hooting as it circled the tree. The order of the day was: stockings, then breakfast, then presents—another rule forgotten in our newly adult household, where coffee and Christmas bread go on all morning, and breakfast has turned into brunch.

The house smells like coffee and bacon, evergreens and wood smoke. We wear comfortable clothes, we eat a lot and talk a lot, we stretch like cats and glory in the day ahead. Some years we're blessed with a long cold spell that gives us solid, smooth ice, and most of us head for the river. Or sometimes there's enough snow to put on our skis at the back door and cross-country ski through the woods. When it's oddly warm, as it has been the past few years, many of us walk off brunch on paths soft and lushly green with moss, now and then seeing partridge berries bright as drops of blood among the leaves.

And, of course, there are always the nappers, the readers, the game players, and the contenders for the annual Nerf Ping-Pong championship. Christmas Day has become a free day. The house is clean, the halls decked, the refrigerator filled with a roast ham and turkey, last night's leftover roast beef, and wild rice salad, the pantry stuffed with bread, fruit, and far too many sweets. Just as it grows dark, people begin to arrive for our traditional open house. Neighbors, relatives, and friends—we never know exactly how many will come; we just put out all the food, light the candles, stoke up the fire, and enjoy ourselves. I hope you will, too. Merry Christmas!

CHRISTMAS EVE SUPPER

MARINATED CHÈVRE WITH PEPPERS

SAGE ROASTED POTATOES

YORKSHIRE PUDDING

HORSERADISH SAUCE

ROAST BEEF

SPINACH WREATH FILLED WITH BABY BEETS

A FULL-BODIED FRENCH BORDEAUX

PINECONE CHRISTMAS CAKE

FROSTED GRAPES

GLACÉ NUTS

CHAMPAGNE

CHRISTMAS EVE SUPPER

The Christmas Eve meal practically cooks itself. The chèvre (goat cheese), pudding batter, spinach wreath, and sweets are all prepared ahead; the beef and potatoes roast together while we are at church. When we get back, it takes only half an hour to cook the pudding and warm up the vegetable wreath while we enjoy chèvre and peppers, presents, and each other.

Below are all the recipes for this menu except the Pinecone Christmas Cake, which is on page 50, and the Glacé Nuts recipe, found on page 42.

MARINATED CHÈVRE WITH PEPPERS

More and more New England farmers seem to be keeping goats for milk and cheese, and local chèvre is easy to find here. If you should have trouble getting it, French chèvre is even more widely available, and you may certainly use it. The combination of milky white cheese and red and green pepper strips makes this as visually appealing as it is delicious. At least a day ahead, prepare the cheese and peppers separately.

To make the cheese: In a container large enough to hold the cheese, mix the rosemary, tarragon, thyme, and garlic. Add the oil and mix. Place the chèvre in the container and coat it with the oil and herbs. Sprinkle with salt and pepper. Cover and refrigerate until an hour or so before serving.

To make the peppers: Place the pepper halves, cut side down, on a foil-lined cookie sheet and broil until the skins are dark brown to black. Put the peppers in a paper bag, close the bag, and let stand until cool.

Skin the peppers, slice them into thin strips, and place in a small container. Cover the pepper strips with the oil and add the garlic, if desired. Cover and refrigerate.

When ready to serve, remove the cheese from the oil and put it on a plate or board. Surround it with the pepper strips and crackers or small slices of the bread. Garnish with herbs, watercress, or olives. The guests can spread the cheese on the crackers or bread and top it with a tangle of pepper strips.

Note: If you have pepper strips left over, return them to the olive oil and use them later. Refrigerated, they will keep for a week or two. When you've used all the peppers, discard the garlic and save the oil for salad dressing.

Makes 8 to 10 servings.

Cheese

- 1 tablespoon dried rosemary
- 2 teaspoons dried tarragon
- ½ teaspoon dried thyme
- ½ clove garlic, minced
- 2 tablespoons virgin olive oil
- 1 log chèvre
  Salt
  Ground black pepper

Peppers

- 1 sweet red pepper, halved, cored, and seeded
- 1 green pepper, halved, cored, and seeded
- ½ cup olive oil
- 1 clove garlic, crushed (optional)
  Crackers or dill bread
  Sprigs of herbs, watercress, or olives (optional)

Marinated Chèvre with Peppers

SAGE ROASTED POTATOES

I like to make these for Christmas because I usually still have beautiful silvery green sage in my otherwise bleak herb garden. If the sage is too shriveled from cold and wind, I simply switch to rosemary. Too tender to survive New England winters, except by the sea, my rosemary grows on the windowsill from November on, filling the room with its delicious piny fragrance.

12–16 **small potatoes (about 2" diameter), peeled**
Butter, softened
Sprigs of sage
Salt
Ground black pepper

If you don't have small potatoes, use larger potatoes, but cut them in halves or quarters. The pieces should all be roughly the same size for uniform cooking. Lightly smear the potatoes with butter. Put the potatoes in the same roasting pan you're using to cook your beef. Tuck sage beneath the potatoes, then season them with salt and pepper.

Roast the potatoes along with the beef. If they are not cooked through or if they need further browning by the time the roast is cooked, transfer them to an ovenproof serving dish and let them cook longer. I would do them with the Yorkshire Pudding in this menu. (If you're doing this recipe by itself, place the potatoes and other ingredients in a 9" × 13" baking dish and bake at 375° for 45 to 50 minutes, or until golden brown and crisp; stir frequently during cooking.)

Garnish the platter or serving dish with more sage.

Makes 8 servings.

YORKSHIRE PUDDING

Most people, I have found, serve either potatoes or pudding, but not both. Well, I tried that, and no matter which one I offered, someone was always disappointed. So now I cook potatoes as well as pudding and find that we all like eating both.

3	eggs
1½	cups milk
1½	cups unbleached flour
¾	teaspoon salt
½	teaspoon ground black pepper
	Beef drippings (from roast beef)
3–4	tablespoons unsalted butter

Put the eggs, milk, flour, salt, and pepper in a blender and process just until the batter is smooth. (Or place the eggs in a large bowl and beat with an electric mixer or by hand until well-blended; beat in the remaining ingredients.)

In a large roasting pan containing the drippings (or in a 9" × 13" pan), melt the butter. Add the pudding batter.

Bake at 450° for 10 minutes, then reduce the heat to 350° and bake for another 15 to 20 minutes, or until the pudding is golden brown and puffy. (Try not to open the oven door during the first 20 minutes of baking.)

Remove the pudding from the oven and cut it into generous squares. Unfortunately, it will collapse within minutes, but there isn't much you can do about that. Just focus instead on the irresistible contrast of texture from crisp and dry to soft and moist—and on the terrific flavor.

Makes 8 servings.

HORSERADISH SAUCE

If ever I needed a reason to indulge in roast beef, it would be to have as a vehicle for this perfect sauce.

1½	cups heavy cream, whipped
½–¾	cup freshly grated horseradish
¼	cup white wine vinegar
2	tablespoons finely chopped scallions
¾	teaspoon salt
	Ground black or red pepper

In a medium bowl, fold together all ingredients. If you make it beforehand, keep refrigerated until you're ready to serve.

Makes about 2½ cups.

ROAST BEEF

Most of us have a favorite cut of beef and a trusted recipe for cooking it. While there is nothing as impressive as a standing rib roast, I usually buy a rib eye because it's easier to slice thin. I buy a good big roast beef (or roast beast, as my son Andrew used to call it), so there will be plenty left over on Christmas Day for our open house. Serve with the delicious horseradish sauce described above.

SPINACH WREATH FILLED WITH BABY BEETS

You can make this into a kind of Della Robbia wreath by adding cooked baby carrots and pearl onions to the spinach ring after you've unmolded it. I usually don't bother, though, because it's pretty enough as it is, simply green with little ruby beets in the center.

Spinach

- 1 cup cottage cheese
- 4 ounces processed Gruyère cheese, diced
- 4 boxes (10 ounces each) frozen chopped spinach, thawed and squeezed dry
- 1 cup coarsely chopped fennel
- 1 cup loosely packed shredded Gruyère cheese (not processed)
- 1 tablespoon lemon juice
- 4 teaspoons minced fresh tarragon or 2 teaspoons dried
- 1 teaspoon ground nutmeg
- ½ teaspoon salt
  Ground black pepper

To make the spinach: Put the cottage cheese in the work bowl of a food processor and process until fairly smooth. Add the diced Gruyère and process again until blended. Add the remaining ingredients. Process again until the mixture is blended.

Generously butter a 1- to 2-quart ring mold and pack it with the spinach mixture. Place the mold in a larger pan. Add about 2 inches of water to the outer pan. Bake at 350° for 30 minutes. (You may also bake the ring along with the beef.)

To make the beets: Place the beets in a medium bowl and microwave on high (100%) for 1 to 2 minutes, or until heated through. (You may also place the beets in a saucepan and heat on the stove for a few minutes.) Add the remaining ingredients. Then toss well.

To serve, unmold the spinach by inverting the mold on a serving plate and lightly tapping the bottom. Be patient—eventually it will come out. I've never had any trouble with this, but if the spinach should decide not to come out in one piece, don't worry; you can very easily push it back together. Fill the center of the ring with the beets and serve immediately.

Beets

- 1–2 cups cooked and peeled baby beets or diced larger beets
- 2–4 tablespoons unsalted butter
- 1–2 tablespoons lemon juice
  Salt
  Ground black pepper

Makes 8 servings.

FROSTED GRAPES

Whenever I hear about sugarplums, I think of these beauties.

Separate the red and green grapes into tiny clusters of 5 to 10 grapes each.

In a small bowl, slightly beat the egg white with a fork to break it up well. Place the sugar on a piece of wax paper or in a small bowl.

Dip each grape cluster into the egg white, coating it thoroughly. Then dip it into the sugar, also making sure to coat it well. Place on a wire rack and allow to dry. Serve the same day.

- 1 small bunch red seedless grapes
- 1 small bunch green seedless grapes
- 1 egg white
- ½ cup granulated or crystallized sugar

Makes enough for 6 to 8 to nibble with dessert.

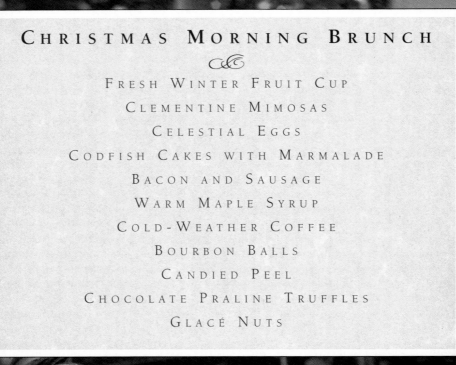

CHRISTMAS MORNING BRUNCH

FRESH WINTER FRUIT CUP

CLEMENTINE MIMOSAS

CELESTIAL EGGS

CODFISH CAKES WITH MARMALADE

BACON AND SAUSAGE

WARM MAPLE SYRUP

COLD-WEATHER COFFEE

BOURBON BALLS

CANDIED PEEL

CHOCOLATE PRALINE TRUFFLES

GLACÉ NUTS

CODFISH CAKES
WITH MARMALADE

You can't get more New England than codfish cakes for a winter breakfast. This is an old family recipe, and it's absolutely delicious with its hint of ginger. All our local fish markets have very good codfish cakes, completely cooked, so all you have to do is pop them in the oven. Just in case you don't have a fish market that carries them, here's the original recipe.

1½	cups flaked cooked codfish
2	cups hot mashed potatoes
2	tablespoons unsalted butter, softened
1	egg
1	egg yolk
2	tablespoons heavy cream
1	teaspoon salt
½	teaspoon ground black pepper
¼	teaspoon grated fresh ginger or ½ teaspoon ground
3–5	tablespoons unsalted butter
1–2	tablespoons canola oil
	Tart marmalade

In a medium bowl, mix the fish, potatoes, and softened butter.

In a small bowl, whisk together the egg and egg yolk, then beat in the cream.

Stir the eggs into the fish mixture. Add the salt, pepper, and ginger. Form the mixture into 8 small cakes. (You can do this the night before; cover the cakes with plastic wrap and refrigerate.)

In a large frying pan over medium heat, melt 2 tablespoons of the butter with ½ tablespoon of the oil. When the butter begins to foam, add the fish cakes in small batches and brown on each side, adding more butter and oil when needed. Drain the cakes on paper towels or pieces of brown paper bags. Keep them warm until needed. Serve with the marmalade.

Makes 8 servings.

EDIBLE CENTERPIECE

For an easy and edible centerpiece, put a beautiful pineapple in the middle of your table. Surround it with apples, tangerines, pears, crab apples, kumquats, and red and green grapes. I usually scatter some nuts around this centerpiece, then tuck in sprigs of laurel, boxwood, rosemary, and cedar. If you like, you can put this all on a round tray—but conceal the edges with greenery.

NEW YEAR'S EVE DINNER FOR TWO

❧

ARTICHOKES MALTAISE

SMOKED SALMON ON DILL BREAD

CHAMPAGNE SCALLOP AND RICE RING

SAUTÉED CHERRY TOMATOES

WATERCRESS SALAD WITH CHAMPAGNE DRESSING

GLAZED ORANGES

CHOCOLATE PRALINE TRUFFLES

CHAMPAGNE

NEW YEAR'S EVE DINNER
FOR TWO

My husband and I have always had a horror of New Year's Eve parties. After all, New Year's Eve is important and deserves more dignity and respect than most people often give it. We usually have a delicious dinner, set the alarm for 11:55, and go to bed early. We wake up in time to open the door wide to welcome in the New Year and have a glass of champagne, a blue-ribbon embrace, and a quiet moment of reflection. One frosty New Year's Eve, Upton put two champagne glasses on the windowsill next to our bed and lowered the bottle out the window on the end of his bathrobe cord. Wonderful—we didn't even have to get out of bed at midnight.

ARTICHOKES MALTAISE

I used to make these artichokes by boiling them for 30 to 40 minutes in a large pot of water to which I added the juice of half a lemon. Now, however, I use the microwave and prepare them in a fraction of the time.

To make the artichokes: Trim each artichoke by cutting the stem flush with the bottom. Cut about 1 inch off the top. Trim all thorns off the tips of the leaves with scissors. Pull off any brown leaves near the base. As you work, rub the cut surfaces with the lemon halves.

Wrap each artichoke tightly in microwave-safe plastic wrap. Place the artichokes side by side on the floor of the microwave and cook on high (100%) for about 10 minutes in a 650- to 700-watt microwave (or for about 15 minutes in a 400- to 500-watt oven). To check for doneness, press the bottom of one of the artichokes with your fingertip. It should give slightly.

Remove the artichokes from the microwave and let them stand for a few minutes. Before unwrapping, prick the plastic with the tip of a knife to release some of the steam.

To make the sauce Maltaise: In a small, deep container (I use a tiny enamel pitcher), very slowly melt the butter and keep it warm.

In a cup, combine and barely heat the lemon juice and orange juice; keep this warm, too.

Have ready a small bowl that fits over a saucepan or the lower half of a double boiler. Put enough water in the pan so that the bowl will rest just *above* the water, not touching it. Bring the water to a boil, then lower the heat so the water barely simmers.

Put the egg yolks in the bowl and position it over the hot water. Beat well with a wire whisk or hand-held electric mixer until the yolks begin to thicken. Beat in 1 tablespoon of the boiling water and keep beating until the yolks again begin to thicken. Repeat, 1 tablespoon at

Artichokes

- 2 artichokes
- 1 lemon, halved

Sauce Maltaise

- ½ cup unsalted butter
- 1 tablespoon lemon juice
- 1 tablespoon orange juice
- 3 egg yolks
- 3 tablespoons boiling water
- ¼ teaspoon soy sauce
- Grated peel of 1 orange
- Pinch of salt
- Pinch of ground red pepper

CHAPTER SIX

NANTUCKET NOEL

from shoppers' stroll to boar's head buffet

It was 10° and pitch black when I left my house well before dawn on December 4, bound for Nantucket Island. By 9:00, when I boarded the ferry in Hyannis, a weak winter sun had risen and so had the wind that whistled through the vast, deserted parking lot. This was a far cry from the summer scene with its crush of cars and crowds. I drove onto the ferry behind a huge flatbed trailer from Canada, which was stacked with layers of Christmas trees and frosted with snow.

Up in the ship's lounge, a handful of travelers nursed their first cups of coffee; a few more were stretched out on hard benches, while one fellow dozed with a Santa's cap tilted crookedly over his forehead. At the bow end of the lounge, a short Christmas tree twinkled; a very small boy stood close to the tree, staring at the shiny balls, a thread of tinsel clinging to his sweater sleeve. The engines began to throb. I zipped up my down jacket, pulled on my wool hat, and went out on deck.

The glare ice was everywhere. Gingerly picking my way along rows of empty deck chairs, I grasped the railing just as we began to pull away from the dock. Across the harbor a wreath hung from the yardarm of a little fishing boat, red ribbons cheerful in the fresh breeze, and I spied a Christmas tree perched on top of the lighthouse. On the ferry, lights were strung from mast to stern, with another lighted tree just outside the pilot house. I hadn't expected to discover signs of Christmas in all these unlikely places!

THE FARAWAY ISLE

Nantucket, a sandy island shaped like a cradle, lies 30 miles southeast of Hyannis across Nantucket Sound. Sheltering its harbor is an 8-mile barrier beach that stretches from southwest to southeast, constantly sculpted, eroded, and silted over by wind and water. Geography books will tell you Nantucket is the work of a giant glacier; Nantucketers will tell you instead about Maushope, a giant Cape Cod Indian, who woke up with sand in his moccasins. In a rage, he kicked them off. The one that landed closest to shore became Martha's Vineyard, and the distant one became Nantucket, Algonguian for "the faraway isle." Maushope is also responsible for the fog that so often wraps the island: They say it is smoke from his great pipe.

There was no fog today, but the rough water below looked milky. I thought of the shifting shoals that encircle Nantucket and the many ships that had foundered nearby, earning this island the name "Graveyard of the Atlantic." Suddenly Nantucket seemed distant and cold, and I found myself remembering the two storms that ravaged Nantucket in the summer and fall of 1991—Hurricane Bob at the end of August, followed two months later by the even fiercer No-Name Storm. I began to wonder if it was only the mainland that was slipping away behind me and not part of the twentieth century as well.

THE SHOPPERS' STROLL

The occasion for my visit was the 19th annual Nantucket Christmas Stroll. The first stroll was held during the energy crisis of the early 1970s, when most New England towns did not use Christmas lights. To make up for a dark Main Street, Nantucket shopkeepers decided to stay open late one Friday night in mid-December and turn Main Street into an island party. There would

be mulled cider, cranberry punch, cheese, and cookies. There were carolers and, of course, a Santa Claus. That first year, everyone turned out, shopped, ate, and visited—and had such a good time that they resolved to repeat the stroll the following year. Now the stroll has grown from a simple island affair to a tourist attraction, and by Labor Day, all of the 1,350 island guest rooms are already booked.

All along Main Street, trees a little taller than my head were festooned with big, old-fashioned, colored lights (not yet lighted) and a wild diversity of decorations. A tree commemorating Hurricane Bob, and another in honor of the No-Name Storm, were decked in treasures salvaged from surf and wind—cans, shells, plastic nozzles, feathers, toys, skates'-egg cases, fishing net, and rope.

Other trees were decorated by elementary school classes. I particularly liked Grade Three's, which was strung with pretzel ornaments and handwritten wishes: "I wish there is no more crime," "I wish that all the factories in the world will not pollute the air," and "I wish the hole erth was free." The Campfire Girls had decorated one tree with reindeer fashioned from cardboard toilet-paper rolls and pipe cleaners, and everyone seemed to find decorative ways to make scallop shells into ornaments.

But the tree I hoped would win a prize was the one decorated by the Salt Marsh Senior Center. It was covered with pierced ornaments that looked like Mexican silver, and when I got up close I could read "Morton" and "Swanson" embossed on the aluminum. TV dinner trays!

Several small, enticing Main Street shops lured me inside. People were busy with last-minute touches but not too busy to chat.

"You must be dreading the crowds this weekend," I said sympathetically to one shopkeeper.

He looked at me as if I were crazy. "No. Why?"

"Well, so many people coming, isn't it an intrusion?"

"Oh no! Not at all. We love it. We love the stroll."

TOWARD PETTICOAT ROW

The severe cold had literally nipped late-blooming roses in the bud as well as hollyhocks and chrysanthemums, and now they stood stiffly, still colorful, beside doorways and picket fences garlanded with Christmas greens. I headed for Center Street, once called Petticoat Row. In former days, Nantucket women maintained successful shops on this lane, powering the island economy and improving their own finances (unheard of, for women in those days). Shops are still bustling on Center Street, though today not all are run by women. And instead of providing household staples like their predecessors, these galleries and shops specialize in handmade jewelry, exotic furnishings, and one-of-a-kind creations.

This is where I discovered the sailors' valentines, made by seamen long ago for their sweethearts. These valentines were intricate concoctions of shells gathered on faraway shores and kept in cramped shipboard quarters, then painstakingly glued into delicate, three-dimensional hearts. I tried to imagine these frail, translucent shells cradled in rough sailors' hands, and the gentleness this conjured up made my throat ache. On a typical voyage a sailor might be at sea for four or five years—a very long time to be away from your sweetheart.

WALKING THE SHORE

Leaving town toward evening, I headed toward the south shore, the one facing Spain, 8 miles of beach and pounding surf. The recent storms had drastically accelerated the erosion of the bluffs and Sankaty Head Light—a National Historic Landmark that has warned sailors off the southern shoals for 141 years—now looked to be in peril.

Anyone who walks this wild shore must end up feeling small and impermanent, yet full of wonder for Nantucket's survival. The beach was clean of flotsam, offering instead tangled skates'-egg cases, solitary scallop shells, and infant quahog shells no bigger or tougher than my fingernail. I filled my pockets with a selection of shells and turned away from the relentless wind.

Back in town, where twilight and glowing windows increased the illusion of nineteenth-century life, the streets were deserted. The majestic Main Street elms made lacy arches above the old street lamps as the darkness settled fast. A separation of 30 miles from so-called civilization, with its excess of halogen lights and pulsing traffic, makes an immeasurable difference. Nantucket's winter quiet is *quiet,* and her dark is *dark.*

ONE NIGHT IN A CAPTAIN'S HOUSE

At the upper end of Main Street, captains' houses face one another across cobblestones that are said to have arrived on the island as ships' ballast. These houses are dignified, close together, and safe-looking. Protected gardens are tucked behind, and towering holly trees separate neighbor from neighbor. (It seems to me that Nantucket hollies, like Nantucket elms, grow taller and better than their kin on the mainland, perhaps to make up for the scruffy and sparse growth elsewhere on the island.) Three very handsome brick houses in a row, known as the three bricks, bear the family name Starbuck on their brass nameplates.

Across the street from the Starbucks, but no less mighty, stand white clapboard twins with Greek Revival pediments and columns. But the more typical captains' houses are shingled, unpretentious, with many-paned windows and lowish ceilings, picket fences, and rose trellises. Peeking through the tied-back curtains, I felt as if I could enter, for a moment, these lived-in, warm, worn rooms.

The house I stayed in was one of these. Appearing modest in size from the street, it stretched far back—a good house for a plentiful family. The staircase described a graceful curve up the front hall.

When I put my hand on the banister, I noticed a curious little ivory button in the center of the newel post. "A mortgage button," said my hostess, Lyn. "As soon as you paid off your mortgage, the bank would put in the button." No refinancing, I guess.

This house, like so many on Nantucket, doubles as a bed-and-breakfast and, like all the others, had been booked in advance for the stroll. Lyn's daughter had given me her room, making me really feel like family, as if I truly belonged.

THE CHRISTMAS HOUSE TOUR

One of the annual features of the Christmas Stroll is the Christmas House Tour, held to benefit the Nantucket public schools. The year of my visit, the tour included five very different old houses and the Methodist Church. A series of luminaria—paper bags with candles flickering inside them—lighted my way along the narrow streets all the way down to the harbor.

Gazing out beyond the close-flanked buildings that hugged the harbor side, I spotted what may be the best Christmas decoration in the world. One lone dory nudged a harbor mooring, and inside the dory was a plump and brightly lighted tree. As it bobbed on the gentle ripples, its colored lights sent darts of shimmering reflections across the languid water. Harbor lights, luminaria, and the rocking Christmas tree were a quiet, twinkling prelude to tomorrow's stroll.

"LET THE STROLL BEGIN!"

By Saturday morning, Nantucket town was humming. Main Street had been blocked off to vehicles. In the crowd that filled the street, I began to spot a few lightship baskets—traditional wicker-handled "Nantucket purses" that are topped with scrimshaw. Full-length furs appeared, a sure sign that visitors had arrived. At 11:30, the town crier met the ferry and welcomed the disembarking crowd in a most personal yet dignified manner. Like the Pied Piper, he led them to the foot of Main Street.

The town crier is the matinee idol of the stroll. He wears an eclectic outfit that at first glance looks a little like Ben Franklin's, with a tricorn hat, black swallowtail coat, and ruffly jabot. But this being chill Nantucket, the crier adds touches appropriate to the North Atlantic—a wonderful scarlet vest, a thick duofold turtleneck, and (he confided on the sly) several layers of long johns. His black shoes look like sturdy traditional wingtips, devoid of Ben Franklin–style buckles. He wears his black cape with splendid flair except when it rains, as it did a few years ago. (At the end of *that* stroll, the soaking cape weighed over 50 pounds.)

It is the crier's privilege to open the stroll. Shortly after noon, we all began to gather around him, our eyes fixed on the hands of the Unitarian Church clock. At exactly 12:30, he jubilantly rang his British air raid warden's bell and shouted, "Let the stroll begin!"

FROM CAROLERS TO PIGLETS

Eight accomplished Nantucket Chamber Music carolers, resplendent in velvet bonnets, cloaks, top hats, and tailcoats, climbed up on the flatbed in the middle of Main Street and filled the street with song. They were followed by island singer Gary Mehalick and his guitar, the joyful Appalachian Brass Quintet, seven young Nantucketers from the St. Paul's Youth Choir, and the Community Bell Choir.

Although people gathered around the stage, they left plenty of room up front for all the children. In this safe gathering, even quite small children wandered independently from the music to the countless other surprising and unplanned stroll attractions. Some of the tots were transfixed by the sight of an almost life-size Tyrannosaurus rex; others paused as a woolly mammoth went swaying through the crowd. And many of the children stopped to chat with a bunny puppet.

Through the midst of the crowd, one woman carried a large white goose that every now and then "produced" a golden egg. (This the woman wordlessly presented to anyone nearby.) A pair of live piglets wearing Santa hats and little jackets trotted along on leashes. An enormous elf dressed in green velvet and very long,

green, pointy-toed elf shoes came and went, dispensing candy from a huge sack.

The town crier was still the focal point of much activity. People lined up to have their pictures taken standing next to him. (It was just like having your picture taken on Santa's lap, only instead of a fat elf, this was an island dignitary.) The Nantucketers called out to each other, swapped children, and flowed from cluster to cluster. I overheard two boys discussing their report cards with one of the policemen and watched some kids admire their own decorations on the trees. A shrill rendition of "Jingle Bells," chirped by Alvin and the Chipmunks, came from the ambulance parked nearby.

THE TALKING
CHRISTMAS TREE

At the bottom of Main Street, I noticed people standing in front of a plain, barely decorated tree, and I went down to investigate. A little girl in a bright purple jacket walked by the tree—and just as she did, the most startling thing happened. The tree *spoke*.

"Hello," it said. "Hello, little girl in the purple jacket."

The little girl stopped and looked around her, confused.

"Hello, little girl, don't be afraid. This is the tree."

The little girl looked at the tree quickly. One hand flew to her mouth in amazement. The other reached for her mother's reassuring grasp. Smiling, the mother put her arm around the child.

The tree spoke again: "Yes, I'm the tree. Right here. Would you like to shake my branch?"

The little girl's eyes were very big now. Mother and child moved closer to the tree. Very tentatively, the little girl reached out and shook a branch.

"That's it," said the tree. "How do you do? Merry Christmas! Now, what's your name?"

"Thoothee," whispered the little girl.

"Susie?" asked the tree.

Susie nodded.

"Well now, Susie, what would you like for Christmas?"

Susie lifted the hand from her mouth, took a deep breath and started in. I was smiling so hard my teeth got cold, and at the same time, I felt a catch in my throat.

After Susie had finished, a bunch of boys walked by and the tree called out, "Hey, Charlie. Charlie Johnson. Aren't you going to introduce me to your friends?"

The boys stopped dead in their tracks, and one of them (Charlie, presumably) turned beet red and muttered into the green branches. It went on like this all afternoon. The talking tree knew almost everyone, even two fifth-grade teachers whom he chided for "hanging around talking to a stupid tree."

SANTA AT THE BANK

Santa arrived in a horse-drawn carriage, jingle bells jingling, and held court inside the Pacific Bank. Outside, a queue of strollers snaked for several blocks. The stroll ended at twilight with everyone singing carols in front of the bank, tired children sitting against each other under the Christmas tree, looking up at the branches, mesmerized by the twinkling lights.

From the bank many headed to the Methodist Church next door for a candlelight ecumenical service of readings and carols. Walking home along Main Street that night, I looked back where so many of us had thronged hours before, astonished to find it neat as a pin. There wasn't a single trace of the 4,000 strollers.

THE BOAR'S HEAD BUFFET

I returned to Nantucket two weeks later for the annual Boar's Head Buffet at the Jared Coffin House and the Celebration of Christmas—Nantucket's pageant. Jared Coffin, one of Nantucket's leading ship owners, built the first three-story house on the island in 1845. Because it was made of brick, this mansion survived the Great Fire of 1846 and has been an inn ever since that time, passing through many owners. In 1976, the Nantucket Historical Trust sold the house to its current owners, Phil and Peg Read.

Every year the Reads host a boar's head buffet, with family readings and rituals first, in the parlor of the Jared Coffin House. The dining room can accommodate about 80, and that's how many of us were there, with about an equal mix of guests and island residents. The house was trimmed with ribboned garlands of boxwood, laurel, and frosted fruit. Double wreaths hung in every window, and a large tree stood beside the silver wassail bowl in the back drawing room. In the adjoining front parlor, a good fire snapped smartly.

THE YULE LOG LEGEND

A little after 6:00 P.M., Phil and Peg, with their grown children, Amanda and Christopher, welcomed us with seasonal readings and personal remembrances. Instantly, we felt that we had become a part of their family Christmas. Phil introduced his mother and told us in a straightforward way that went right to the heart that his father had just passed away, and so this Christmas was bittersweet. He explained the tradition of the yule log, which, if kept burning all night, would prevent Satan from entering. He reminded us that the log must be taken from our land or a neighbor's, and above all, that it must never be bought. And he toasted his fire, as he does every year, by tossing a cup of wassail into the flames and saying:

"May the fire of this log warm the cold; may the hungry be fed; may the weary find rest; and may all enjoy Heaven's peace. Be thou well!" The fire hissed and sparked, and the flames leapt up.

According to our host, the boar's head feast is based on a venerable English tradition with Biblical roots. In the 80th Psalm Satan is called "the boar out of the wood." According to this lore, presenting the boar's severed head at Christmastime proves that Satan has been defeated by the newborn Child.

There was a bit of commotion in the hallway, and we all turned to look. In came the boar's head surrounded by rosemary and bay, held high on a platter by chef Bob McGowan. The rest of the kitchen staff followed him, holding aloft platters of beef Wellington, Nantucket scallops, roasted hams and geese with cranberries and cherries, braces of quail served on a mirror, smoked salmon, boiled lobster, oysters, and clams on ice. We all followed the food into the dining room, where two life-size angels carved in ice presided over the banquet table.

It was a noisy, merry, unpretentious feast with lots of table hopping. Phil came to ours and told me more about the boar's head tradition—but we were too busy eating to think much of Satan's downfall. We realized, however, that we would have to leave room for the captain's cranberry tart, which occupied a place of honor on the sideboard, its cranberries glistening like garnets. And when it was finally served, we quickly discovered that it tasted as good as it looked. I vowed that I wouldn't leave the island until I had wrested the recipe from our chef. Fortunately, Bob McGowan was more than willing to pass it along, with a few special notes for those who can't get freshly picked Nantucket cranberries.

Jared Coffin House

Chef McGowan selects the ripest, juiciest cranberries from the fall harvest for his delicious tart. But you can buy frozen cranberries any time of year, if you want to enjoy this treat out of season.

CAPTAIN'S CRANBERRY TART

To make the filling: In a large bowl, combine all ingredients and mix well. Cover and chill for 2 hours.

To make the crust: In a large bowl, mix the flour, sugar, and salt. Using 2 knives or a pastry blender, cut in the butter until the pieces resemble coarse meal.

Sprinkle with 1 tablespoon of the water and gently mix in with a fork. Continue to add water, 1 tablespoon at a time, until the dough is moist enough to hold together when pressed; try not to add more water than needed.

Form the dough into a ball. Cut in half and flatten each piece into a disk. Wrap in plastic and refrigerate for at least 1 hour.

Working on a lightly floured surface, roll out each piece of dough into approximately an 11-inch circle. Fit 1 piece into a 9-inch pie pan. Add the cranberry mixture.

Cut the second piece of dough into ½-inch strips. Use the strips to form a lattice top over the filling. Trim the edges and flute as desired.

Bake at 325° for 1½ hours. Let cool to room temperature before serving.

Serves 6 to 8.

Filling

2	pounds cranberries
1	Granny Smith apple, peeled, cored, and diced
1	cup sugar
¼	cup orange liqueur
	Grated rind and juice from 1 lemon
2	tablespoons cornstarch
¼	teaspoon salt

Crust

2	cups unbleached flour
	1 tablespoon sugar
	Pinch of salt
½	cup unsalted butter, chilled
	Ice water

THE PAGEANT

Sunday evening, every pew was filled in the graceful cold "summer" sanctuary of the Congregational Church.

On Nantucket, each church is in fact two churches, a lofty summer church and an easier-to-heat winter church. The pageant is so popular that it is held in the larger accommodations, and everyone is instructed to bundle up. Inside, the altar was transformed: A staging had been set up—covered with evergreens—and a bare-branched beach plum bush was the stable. This "pageant to end all pageants" is different every year, according to the director. When my friend Lyn directed it, she told me, she brought on three queens *and* three kings. The presents delivered to Mary included a homespun gown, lullabies, and chicken noodle soup.

This year, there were lots of little angels, animals with paper mâché heads, shepherds and kings, and the holy family—a *real* family with a real, 2-month-old baby girl (which seemed exactly right to me on this island where women have traditionally been movers and shakers). Readers narrated the words of Herod, Isaiah, Amos, and the Gospel, and the Community Chorus, 40 voices strong, made the church vibrate with carols.

The last of the carols was "Silent Night." As the music rose in the chill air of the summer church, candlelight spread from person to person, and a star of only light, no substance, was projected above the manger and sheltering beach plum.

BEAUTY FROM THE BOGS

The traditional cranberry Christmas wreath, shown on page 86, was created by Peg Read to hang on the door of the Jared Coffin House. Since the house stands at the most prominent site at the end of Center Street, the wreath is highly visible. The ingredients needed include: five 12-ounce bags of fresh cranberries; three or four boxes of round, wooden toothpicks; 16-inch Styrofoam wreath form, needle-nose pliers, pine boughs (white pine is nice), florist's pins, wire for hanging, and an all-weather bow. If you can enlist the help of friends or family, ask for volunteers. Stabbing toothpicks into cranberries is a perfectly enjoyable occupation for at least one long New England winter's evening.

Wrap wire around the top of the wreath form to make a hanging loop. Mark the area on the form that will be covered by the pine boughs, as shown in the illustration at right. (This is the part of the wreath that doesn't need to be covered with cranberries.)

Break some toothpicks in half and insert them in firm cranberries. (Throw away any cranberries that feel mushy.) The cranberries on half-toothpicks make up the inner and outer rows of the wreath.

Using the needle-nose pliers, attach a row of cranberries to the top inside of the frame (position A). Attach a second row to the outside edge of the frame at position B. Be sure to crowd the cranberries closely together, and push them in firmly with the pliers.

Insert whole toothpicks in enough cranberries to form one row and attach them to the form in a center row (C). Then insert rows D and E, above and below the center row—but break off part of the toothpicks. (By gradually decreasing the size of toothpicks in each row, you give the wreath a mounded effect.)

Continue filling in with additional rows, making the toothpicks shorter and shorter as you work toward the inner and outer edges.

Cover the base of the wreath with pine boughs, attaching them with florist's pins. Fasten the bow and hang the wreath on the front door. If a few cranberries become soft or discolored, just pull out the toothpicks and replace them. Also, you can spray all the cranberries with clear lacquer to make them last longer. The wreath on the Jared Coffin House usually lasts a month or more.

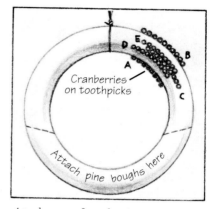

Attach rows of cranberries using toothpicks. Fill in with pine boughs to cover the marked area.

bud, slide it about ½ inch in on a green branch and press it in place. Hold for a second until the glue dries.

4. Distribute about 6 roses of each color on the half of the tree facing you. Then turn the tree around and distribute roses on the other half.

5. Take small bunches of burgundy broom bloom or other delicate dried flowers and place them randomly among the roses.

6. Now add pearls or shiny beads. Place a drop of glue on the tip of a branch and attach beads one at a time. (Hold the strand near a branch, then touch the end bead with a drop of glue. Place the glued bead on the end of the branch, then cut the bead from the strand so it sticks to the end of the branch.) Put on as many beads as you think you need.

7. To make the bows yourself, see "How to Tie a Florist's Bow" on page 133. Scatter the little bows around the tree, securing each with a drop of glue.

8. Cut a slit in the lace on the radius and slide it around the base of the tree. Arrange the folds of lace to hide the slit.

MINI CHRISTMAS GIFTS

You can make each of these gifts in less than an hour. They are perfect for people you'd like to remember at Christmas. And they're nice to have on hand for people who pop in unexpectedly.

CINNAMON STICK PLACECARD HOLDERS

These unusual placecard holders look great on any holiday table, regardless of the centerpiece. It's easier to make these if you have a placecard on hand for measuring. Each holder is a little different, and you may decide to use more or fewer pinecones in yours. Invite your guests to take the holders home as a cinnamon-scented gift of the season.

1. For each holder, tie the cinnamon sticks together around the middle with a rubber band. Arrange the sticks to make a base that lies flat on the table.

2. Cover the rubber band by wrapping it with ribbon.

3. Glue a few tiny pinecones on top. (Cones should not extend to the end of the cinnamon sticks.)

4. Decorate the bundles with your choice of fern and cedar greenery, blossoms, berries, or more tiny cones.

5. Cut the cards or stationery into rectangles measuring 2" × 1¼". In the upper left corner of each card, glue a pinecone or rosebud, a sprig or two of nursery fern or cedar, or a few berries. Insert cards down in between the cinnamon sticks.

Decorate the placecard holders with pinecones and greens and insert card as shown.

Materials

Short (3") cinnamon sticks (5 for each holder)

Rubber bands

⅛" wide ribbon

Glue gun

Tiny pinecones

Preserved nursery fern or fresh cedar; dried rosebuds, starflowers, or other blossoms; and rose hips or pepperberries

White placecards or heavy stationery

CINNAMON STICK MANTEL SPRAY

Elizabeth Timmins, an herbalist and designer, made one of these for Madeleine DiCicco, and then Madeleine made one for me. You can make these sprays as large or small as you like, and please don't feel limited to cinnamon sticks. (Madeleine says that birch twigs are just as wonderful as cinnamon.)

1. Fasten the cinnamon sticks together around the middle with the rubber band. Place the bundle on a flat surface and slightly fan out the ends of the sticks on each side. (Make sure the bundle is resting securely on your work surface; you don't want it to fall over after it's decorated.) Cover the rubber band with the ribbon and tie the ribbon into a bow in front.

2. Slide the cut ends of the sprigs or greens under the rubber band, arranging them so they fill in and soften the cinnamon sticks. Make sure they give both sides of the spray a pleasing shape. The sprigs or greens should not extend out quite as far as the cinnamon sticks. Glue the sprigs in place.

3. Glue on a little sea lavender and dried flowers. Add rosebuds, pinecones, or berries.

4. Arrange a small amount of the Spanish moss in the center of the bow to resemble a nest and add the bird.

Materials

10–14 long (1½') cinnamon sticks

Rubber band

¾"–1" wide ribbon, 2½ yards

Sprigs of spruce or fir or preserved greens

Glue gun

Sea lavender

Assorted dried flowers (such as broom bloom, baby's-breath, starflowers)

Dried rosebuds, tiny pinecones, or berries

Small handful of Spanish moss

Small artificial bird

HOLIDAY BOBECHES

These are tiny wreaths covered with small dried flowers, shells, and berries. They're the perfect seasonal addition to your candlesticks. Although glass bobeches are often placed at the base of candles to catch the drippings, the unique little wreath versions you make yourself will do just as well.

I sometimes make these for myself out of living plant material. The only problem with those is that they don't last more than a few days. If you intend these as gifts, it's better to use the dried material. Make at least a set of two for dinner candles or make one for a big, fat candle (include the candle and a saucer as part of the gift package).

1. Make a small "donut" out of the base material. To make sure the hole in the center is the right size, first trace the bottom of a standard

Materials

Base material (thin Styrofoam, thick cardboard, foamboard, or even an old curtain ring)

Glue gun

Dried mosses

Assorted small dried flowers and herbs, berries (especially rose hips and pepperberries), tiny pinecones, and dried delicate pods or shells

candlestick on the material. (If you're using a curtain ring, all you need to do is find one that's the right diameter to fit around the bottom of the candle.) Then draw a second circle that is about ¼ inch larger than the ring in the center. Cut out the circle in the center, then cut around the outside circumference. That will leave a "donut" of base material that's about ¼ inch wide—just enough space to glue on the other materials.

2. Glue on a layer of moss, extending it over the inside edge of the hole just enough to hide the base of the candles.

3. Glue on tiny flowers, herbs, berries, pinecones, pods, and/or shells, arranging them to cover the outside and top of the base. When it's finished, your bobeche will look like a little wreath. Just slip a candle through the center, insert the candle in a candle holder, and adjust the bobeche at the base.

LIVING BOX TREE

These tiny trees (shown on page 100) are perfect for people in hospitals or nursing homes, or for anyone who doesn't have a standard tree with ornaments.

1. Wet the floral foam and set it in the saucer. (If you're using a saucer that has no prongs, tape the foam to the saucer on all 4 sides with florist's tape.)

2. Roughly shape the block into an oval by shaving the top corners with a knife. Put the saucer on the lazy Susan, if desired.

3. Remove the bottom inch or two of leaves from a 4- to 5-inch sprig of boxwood. Insert the boxwood stem into the bottom of the foam block, just high enough for the branch to extend beyond the saucer to form the "trunk."

4. Decide on a good length for the bottom branches (some people prefer fat trees, others skinny ones). Cut 4 branches and insert them parallel to the working surface, roughly equidistant from one another. They will guide you as you work around the bottom row, filling in that row entirely. Repeat the process on the next 2 rows. (On each row, first insert the 4 guides, then fill in the row with horizontal boxwood sprigs.)

5. Insert a top piece of boxwood (about 7 inches long) so it sticks out the top center of the foam block. This will give you an idea of the shape of your tree.

6. On the 4th row, begin to slightly angle the branches toward the top. (From now on, each row will point increasingly upward.) You should begin to slightly lengthen the branches as well, so that by the time you get to the top few rows, they will hug the top 7-inch branch. Your tree should be bushy and full, with no floral foam peeking through.

7. Now you're ready to decorate the tree. If desired, spray some of the berries gold (see "Spray Paint Cautions" on page 106). Wire them and the bows to the florist's picks and jab them into the tree.

Materials

1 block of floral foam (4" × 3" × 9")

Florist's saucer, 5"–6" in diameter (preferably one with prongs)

Florist's tape (optional)

Paring knife

Lazy Susan (optional)

Several big bunches of boxwood

Gold spray paint (optional)

Rose hips or other red berries

20–30 little bows (or make them using 10" of ¼" wide ribbon per bow; see directions on page 133)

Florist's wire

3–4 dozen florist's picks

CHAPTER EIGHT

SPECIAL GIFTS
TO
QUILT, STITCH & KNIT

the magic of busy hands

~

My husband, Upton, is
the needleworker in the Brady house. While I can
sew on a button, let down a hem, darn a sock,
turn a collar (a New England custom that *doubles*
the life of a shirt), I tremble at the mention of a
pattern. He, on the other hand, has mastered the
intricacies of slipcovers, argyle socks, smocked
baby dresses, you name it. And wonderful though
it is to have a resident seamster, it can also be a
little daunting.

During the energy crisis in the 1970s, we shut
down our huge old converted coal furnace and
heated half our house with an efficient little wood

stove. This would've worked better if the living room had not once been a porch with a 15-foot ceiling and no insulation. Keeping our hands busy seemed to keep us warmer, so we took up knitting.

Don't laugh, it works. It was depressing to hear Upton's needles rapidly clicking away while I laboriously looped and slipped, but I *did* finally finish a thick Norwegian sweater for my daughter, Sarah, a Christmas present given several years after it was begun. I keep thinking I'll make another, but then I remember someone's observation that watching me knit was like watching a beginner play a strenuous and exhausting game of basketball, and I confess that's the way it *felt,* too. So these days, instead of knitting to keep warm, I'm more likely to bake cookies or work on a wreath or two.

HOLIDAY HANDIWORK

The projects here are not excruciatingly difficult, Upton tells me. But, the directions are written for people who know how to quilt, stitch, knit, and follow patterns, and these projects take longer to finish than the others in this book. They are also winners. If you *are* someone who can knit or sew, and the patterns here catch your fancy—well, I just wish I were on your Christmas list.

QUILTED CHRISTMAS STOCKING

When I asked my friend Bobbie Ward—who designed these stockings—how long it takes to make one, she laughed. "A week of evenings." When I asked for specifics, she said, "About 6 hours. But you wouldn't just sit down and make a stocking straight, without doing something else, would you?"

Well, probably not—and besides, who can? So choose a rocker by the fire, claim it as your own, and enjoy your "week of evenings" making a quilted stocking.

1. To make a standard-size quilted stocking, enlarge the pattern on the opposite page and transfer it to heavy paper or cardboard (see the photocopying directions in "How to Enlarge a Pattern" on page 40). If you want a stocking that is larger or smaller than the one shown, cut out a pattern from newspaper, experimenting with different shapes and sizes until you're satisfied with the basic form. Trace it on heavy paper or cardboard.

2. Use the pattern to cut 2 stocking shapes from the batting, Therolane, or felt—one will become the front of the stocking, the other the back. Lay them on a flat surface. Be sure to reverse the batting for the back, so the heels face each other.

3. *To make the front:* Lay the stenciled Saint Nicholas or other decorative panel (*right side up*) on top of the batting as shown in the illustration on the opposite page. Use a few straight pins to hold it in place.

Materials

Heavy paper or thin cardboard

Newspaper (optional)

½ yard very thin cotton batting, Therolane, or felt

1 stenciled Saint Nicholas panel (pattern on page 105) or other printed panel

Straight pins

Small pieces and strips of fabric

¼ yard plain fabric (optional)

½ yard lining fabric (optional)

Braids, ribbon, or lace (optional)

4. You will attach all future strips of fabric in the order of their numbers as shown at right. And they will all be attached by the "sew and flip" method. To start, lay strip 1 (*right side down*) on top of the stenciled panel; line up their raw edges (at the right-hand side of the stenciled panel).

5. Pin in place, then stitch through both layers of fabric and the batting to hold the strip in place. (It's up to you whether you want to do the stitching by hand or with a sewing machine.)

6. Trim the seam allowance to ¼ inch. Then flip strip 1 so the right side is exposed; the stitching will not be visible. Continue in the same way until strips 2 through 7 are sewn in place. (Don't worry if strips overhang the batting edge; they will all get trimmed later. And if at any time you misjudge the size of a strip and it doesn't cover the batting, just add another piece of fabric. This is, after all, patchwork, and you can control the design.)

7. When you get to the heel, lay down strip 8 and pin it to the batting. Attach strip 9 as you did the others. Then attach strip 10. Turn under the top edge of strip 10 (where it abuts strip 7; neatly topstitch it to the batting; you *will* see these stitches).

8. Finish the toe by laying down strip 11 and pinning it in place. Add strip 12 and finish off its right-hand raw edge by turning it under and topstitching it down next to strips 9 and 10.

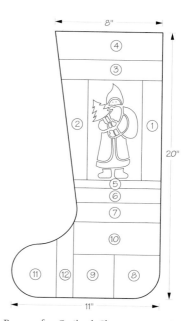

Pattern for Quilted Christmas Stocking (front).

9. *To make the back:* The back can be as fancy or as plain as you want it to be. If you simply cut the back from 1 piece of material, anchor it to the batting with some stitches along the top edge and also from the heel to the toe. If you prefer to strip-piece the back, use larger pieces of fabric and follow the order indicated in the illustration at right.

10. *To assemble the stocking:* Trim all the excess fabric from the front and back, following the shape of the batting. Put right sides together and sew with a scant ½-inch seam allowance, leaving the top open.

11. Trim the seam to about ¼ inch and turn the stocking right side out.

12. To give the stocking more body, make a lining: Fold the lining material so its right sides are together. Trace the stocking onto the double thickness and cut it out.

13. Use a ½-inch seam allowance to sew the 2 pieces together, leaving the top of the stocking open.

14. Trim the seam a little. Do not turn the lining inside out; just insert it into the outer stocking through the top, making sure the toe and heel fit together.

15. *To finish the top edge:* Working on the bias, cut a strip of fabric that is 2 inches wide and long enough to go all the way around the top of the stocking (if you're following the dimensions as shown in the illustration on page 119, it would be about 16½ inches long).

16. Place it *right side down* so it's on top of strip 4 in front and strip 2 in back, with the raw edges aligned. Sew it to strip 4, then to strip 2; where the 2 ends of the bias fabric meet, make a neat join.

17. Trim the seam allowance to about ¼ inch. Fold the bias strip over the top of the stocking, turn under the raw edge and slip-stitch it to the lining and batting. (Don't come through to the top fabric with your stitches.)

18. If desired, decorate the stocking with braids, ribbon, or lace. Attach a small loop to the back seam and your stocking is now ready for Santa to fill. Merry Christmas!

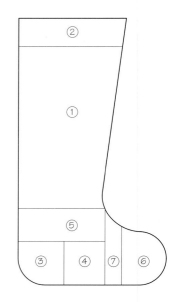

Pattern for Quilted Christmas Stocking (back).

CHICKEN CARDIGAN

Joanne Southworth made this sweater for her granddaughter, Katie, from a North Island design (sweater shown on page 116). You can use the colors of yarn suggested here or create your own color scheme.

The pattern is for size 6—with sizes 8, 10, and 12 indicated in parentheses. For needles, use numbers 4 and 7, or whatever sizes are needed to get a stitch gauge of 5 stitches = 1 inch using knitting worsted yarn. As usual, "K" stands for knit and "P" for purl.

The following directions are for a girl's cardigan with buttonholes on the right front. Work the buttonholes on the left front for a boy's sweater.

Materials

3 (3, 4, 4) 4-ounce skeins main color yarn
10 yards pink yarn
10 yards teal yarn
5 yards yellow yarn
2 yards plum yarn
6 buttons

1. *To make the back:* Using size 4 needles, cast on 66 (69, 72, 75) stitches. Work K2, P1 ribbing for 2½ (2½, 3, 3) inches. Increase 1 (2, 3, 4) stitch evenly across last row of ribbing, so you have 67 (71, 75, 79) stitches.

2. Change to size 7 needles. Working a stockinette pattern (knit 1 row, purl 1 row; knit side is right side of sweater), follow the chicken-wire pattern at right for back. Work until 10 (11, 11½, 12) inches or desired length to underarm.

3. *To make the armhole:* Bind off 3 (4, 4, 5) stitches at the beginning of the next 2 rows. Decrease 1 stitch on each end of every knit row 3 (3, 4, 4) times. Work 29 (29, 31, 33) more rows. Bind off 5 (6, 5, 6) stitches at the beginning of the next 2 rows. Then bind off 5 (5, 6, 6) stitches at the beginning of the next 2 rows and bind off 4 (4, 5, 5) stitches at the beginning of the next 2 rows. Place the remaining 27 stitches on a holder.

4. *To make the left front:* If you're making a boy's cardigan, buttonholes will go on this side. (See instructions below for making the buttonholes.) Otherwise, you can follow the instructions below without any variation.

5. Using size 4 needles, cast on 35 (38, 41, 41) stitches. Work K2, P1 ribbing on first 30 (33, 36, 36) stitches, then seed stitch (K1, P1, K1, P1, K1) on the remaining 5 stitches.

6. Next row: K1, P1, K1, P1, K1 on the first 5 stitches, then K1, P2 across row. Continue this pattern until the ribbing matches the back; increase 2 (1, 0, 2) stitches evenly across last row of ribbing.

7. Change to size 7 needles and work a stockinette pattern following the chicken-wire pattern at bottom of page 122 for front. Work until 10 (11, 11½, 12) inches or desired length to underarm.

8. *To make the armhole:* Bind off 3 (3, 4, 5) stitches at the beginning of the next row. Decrease 1 stitch at the armhole edge every knit row 3 (3, 4, 4) times.

9. Follow the pattern at bottom on page 122, using the appropriate colors, until you reach the neck. Work 13 stitches at front edge, place on holder; work across row. Decrease 1 stitch at neck edge every other row 4 times, and as you work, bind off the shoulders as shown.

10. *To make the right front:* Work the same as left front, only a mirror image, and work 6 buttonholes evenly spaced on button band.

11. *To work the buttonholes:* Work to within 4 stitches of end of row, then bind off 2 stitches firmly; finish row. On next row, K1, P1, and then cast on 2 stitches firmly to make buttonhole. (The first buttonhole should be halfway up the ribbing; the last buttonhole should be midway in the neck ribbing, and the other 4 spaced evenly between.)

12. *To make the sleeves:* Using size 4 needles, cast on 36 (36, 39, 42) stitches. Work K2, P1 ribbing for 2½ (2½, 3, 3) inches. Increase 1 (1, 0, 1) stitch in last row of ribbing.

13. Change to size 7 needles and work next row as follows: K9 (9, 10, 12), P2, K7, P1, K7, P2, K9 (9, 10, 12). Continue to follow grid for chicken-wire pattern for the sleeve (top of page 122) and increase 1

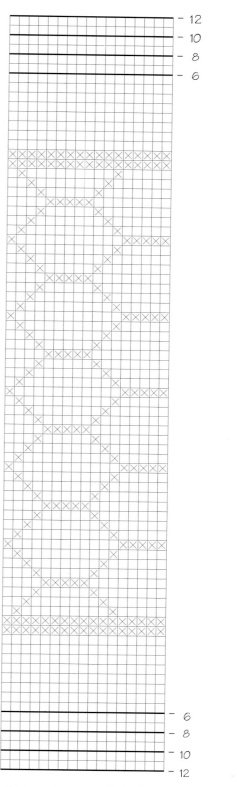

Chicken-wire pattern for back.

stitch each end every 6th row 6 times. Work until the sleeve measures 12 (13, 14, 15) inches or desired length to underarm.

14. *To make the sleeve cap:* Bind off 3 (4, 4, 5) stitches at the beginning of the next 2 rows, then decrease 1 stitch each side every other row until 25 (23, 23, 21) stitches remain. Bind off 3 stitches at the beginning of the next 4 rows. Bind off the remaining 13 (11, 11, 9) stitches.

15. *To finish:* Sew the shoulder seams. Using size 4 needles, pick up and knit stitches on holders and 9 (9, 10, 11) stitches at each neck edge. Work K2, P1 ribbing for 1 inch. Bind off loosely using a much larger needle. Sew seams and weave in ends. Sew on buttons.

Chart for sleeve.

■ = Plum

▨ = Yellow

⊠ = Purl instead of knit (or vice versa on wrong side)

■ = Teal

Hen = Pink

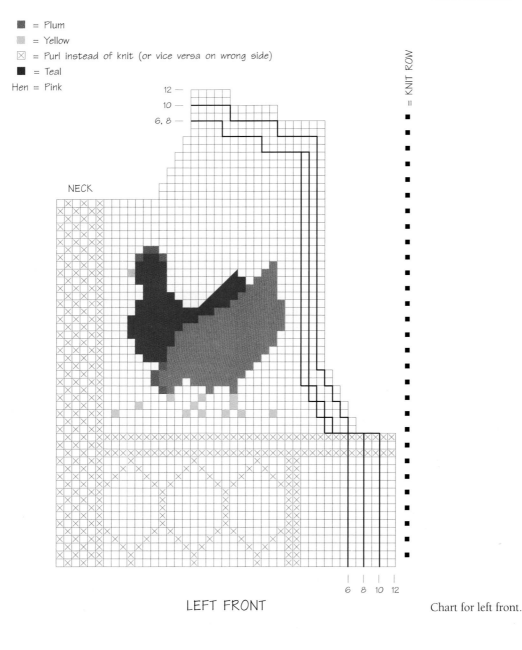

LEFT FRONT

Chart for left front.

QUILLOW

This is, to me, the quintessential New England gift. It is a pure expression of New England ingenuity—a lap-size quilt that has dual uses, because it conveniently folds up to become a pillow. No two quillows need to be anything alike—another bonus for the rugged individualist.

The quillow shown here is the creation of Bobbie Ward, the Bedford neighbor who designed the baby onesie stencil (page 104) and the quilted stocking (page 118). The entire quillow can be made of pieces of preprinted fabric, or it can be pieced together from bits of leftover fabric.

The materials listed at right are for a quilt with finished dimensions of 46½" × 41" (including the border). When folded up into pillow-size, the fabric tucks into a pouch that is 15 inches long and 11½ inches wide.

To make a pieced fabric that follows Bobbie Ward's design, use any strips of fabric that you have on hand, or purchase scrap yardage. Follow the dimensions for cutting, and piece together in the order shown in the illustration on page 124.

In the directions that follow, the side of the quilt with the pillow pouch is called the "backing," and the pieced side is the "front." (The photograph below shows the front of the quillow when it's opened out.)

Materials

Pillow Pouch
Low-loft quilt batting (12" × 15½")
Backing fabric (2 pieces, each 12" × 15½")
Straight pins

Quilt
Low-loft quilt batting (47" × 41½")
Front fabric, pieced or printed (47" × 41½")
Printed backing fabric (47" × 41½")
Binding (use backing fabric, sewn together to make a strip 1¼" in width and 180" long)
Straight pins
Embroidery thread

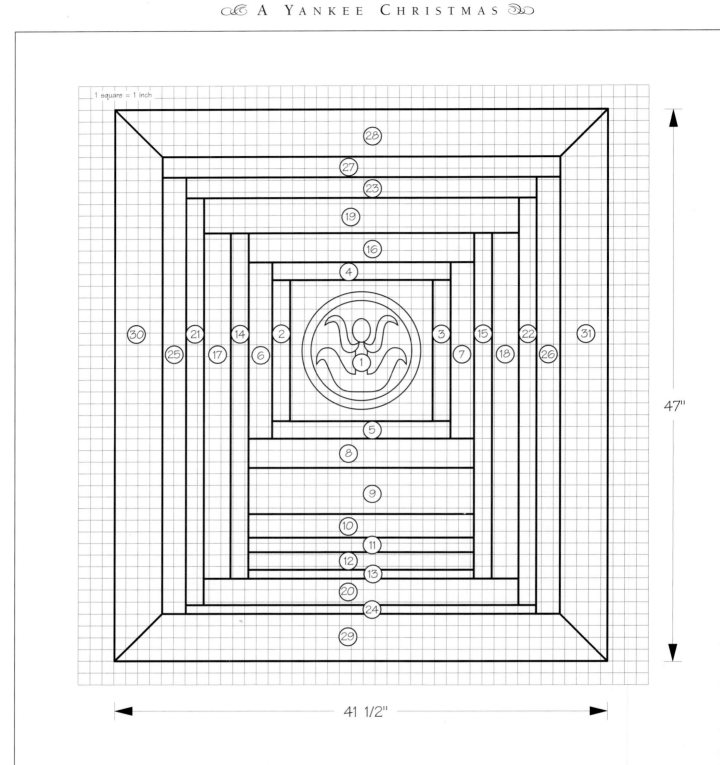

1 square = 1 inch

47"

41 1/2"

Quilting pattern for Quillow.

1. *To make the pillow pouch:* Place the batting on your work surface and cover it with the backing fabric (*right side up*). Lay a second piece of backing fabric on top of that (*right side down*). Pin together the 2 pieces of backing fabric with batting underneath.

2. Sew with a ¼-inch seam allowance all around, leaving an opening of 4 to 5 inches. Trim excess fabric and batting. Then turn the pillow pouch inside out and slip-stitch the opening shut.

3. *To make a pieced quilt front:* Use scraps of fabric to piece together a backing with measurements 47" × 41½". To reproduce Bobbie Ward's design, follow the pattern shown on the opposite page. (The center medallion can be a preprinted or solid block of your choosing.) Cut panels 1 through 31, using the dimensions given in the illustration, and sew together in order, with ¼-inch seams. Note that the dimensions given are for cutting and include seam allowance. (The finished dimensions of each panel will be ½ inch smaller.)

4. *To make a preprinted quilt front:* If you are using preprinted fabric for the front, simply cut a single piece 47" × 41½".

5. *To attach binding:* Turn the front piece right side up. Pin the binding flat around the perimeter, right side down, with the outside edge of the binding flush with the perimeter edge. Sew binding to fabric ½ inch from the outer edge.

6. *To make the quilt:* The first step is to attach the pillow pouch to the backing. Place the batting on your work surface and cover it with the backing (*right side up*). Center the pillow pouch near the top of the backing, 1½ inches down from the upper edge, with the printed side of the pillow right side up (see the illustration at top right). Pin the pillow pouch in position with pins at all 4 corners.

7. Before sewing, you need to "lift" the opening of the pillow pouch to make room for the quilt. To create this extra allowance, unpin 1 of the upper corners (near the edge) and move that side in about 1/8 inch. This will lift the pocket slightly. Repin it.

8. Sew the pocket to the backing (and batting) on 3 sides, leaving the top edge open to form the pouch. Now you are ready to attach the pieced or printed front to the backing.

9. Lay the backing (with the pillow pocket attached) on top of the batting, right side up. Using a scant ½-inch seam allowance, sew across the bottom edge of the backing to secure the backing to the batting.

10. Place the front fabric (*right side down*) on top of the backing. (The pillow is in between the layers at this point, and will come out on top once the quillow is turned.) Pin all 3 layers together.

11. Use a ½-inch seam allowance to sew the layers together and leave a 10-inch opening for turning. (Be careful as you sew the top edge of the quilt not to sew the pillow pouch shut.) Trim the seams and turn the quilt. Close the opening by slip-stitching.

12. When you turn the quilt, ¾ inch of binding will be exposed all around the perimeter. Make a double tuck with the binding to form a ¼-inch border. Iron flat, then slip-stitch the binding to the "backing side" of the quilt.

13. Use embroidery thread to tie the fabric layers together every 6 inches or so, using the technique described in step 9 on page 107.

14. *To fold the pillow:* Lay the quilt flat with the front side up. Fold the left and right sides, as shown at right. Now, fold from the bottom up, 3 or 4 times, guided by the size of the pillow.

15. Turn the pillow pouch inside out, over the folded sections. Plump the pillow—and you're done!

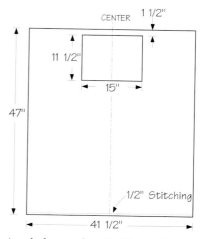

Attach the pouch to Quillow as shown.

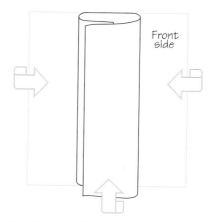

To fold the quilt into a pillow, overlap the sides as shown. Then fold up from the bottom and tuck fabric into the pouch.

CHAPTER NINE

GIFT WRAPPINGS
AND
FINISHING TOUCHES

all ready for the season

What does Christmas look like? The first thing I think of is light—lots of light, flickering in a cold, dark world. Candlelight, starlight, and firelight...lights twinkling in windows, and the glow of Christmas-tree lights.

Every year, when I finish stringing the tiny white lights on our tree, I turn off all the lamps in the living room and just drink in the beauty of that starry tree. And every year, just at that point I ask myself, why not stop now? Why not settle for all lights and no ornaments just this once? But Christmas is also a time of excess, and so I don't stop there—no, I haul out the boxes of ornaments, old friends I haven't seen for 11 months. When the tree is trimmed, I turn out the lamps again and lie underneath it, looking up through the bejeweled branches, once again lost in light.

What Christmas looks like is important. The humblest gift can wear the most exquisite wrapping. Small touches, your touches, will bring Christmas to your house in myriad ways. A garland around a window frame, a wreath, a lighted candle—these are the finishing touches that transform your house into a warm holiday greeting. I put my Christmas cards in a basket on the hall table with ribboned sprigs of holly and rosemary. I tie a brass bell onto one end of a red velvet ribbon and loop the other end over the front door knob. I hang a wreath of fresh greens and rose hips on the front door. And people bring the holiday right in with them.

When wrapping presents or making up a basket, it's good to take your time. Sometimes I do it late at night, when the house is quiet. I like this part, carefully creasing the paper, fluffing up the bow, thinking all the while about the person I'm wrapping the present for. I guess this is the key to Christmas, to celebrate each step and not to consider any one of them a chore, something that *must be done*. I've found that slowing down like that doesn't, in fact, mean you take longer. Because if you love what you are doing, it is effortless. Time is yours—the best gift you have.

BOTTLES AND JARS

Thrifty New Englanders resist buying what they can find for almost-free, especially if it's just a lowly container. We scour flea markets, yard sales, and even the supermarket shelves for jars and bottles. When they're emptied, cleaned, and scoured, they're perfect for holding special Christmas treats.

Down East Soused Shrimp, Mohawk Marinated Mushrooms (both on page 61), jellies, and pickles need to be stored in wide-mouthed jars with tight lids. Although perhaps not works of art, Mason jars are ideal. You can often find them at rummage sales. And if you're lucky, you might even stumble on some of the beautiful old ones. Or next time you're at the market, look for homemade-style spaghetti sauces and salsas in attractive jars all ready for you to recycle. You can spruce up any jar with a snappy label or by tying a bright piece of calico over the lid.

Homemade herb vinegars and oils, bath oils, after-shave splashes, rum shrubs, and the like all must have suitable bottles with caps or corks. Many fancy kitchen stores and craft stores carry corks in assorted sizes.

Here are some bottles that look handsome without their labels: Tabasco sauce, Roland capers, Crosse & Blackwell mint sauce, Atlantic clam juice, Rose's lime juice, A.1. steak sauce, Casa Fiesta hot pepper sauce, Pommery raspberry vinegar (my favorite).

"FLOURISHING EXOTIC" IN NEW ENGLAND HOMES

In 1832, Charles Follen, a German teacher at Harvard, was the first New Englander to cut a Christmas tree, bring it inside, and decorate it. Both his wife and a guest exuberantly recorded this event. Eighty-four wax tapers burned brightly on the outer branches and the fir was heavy with baskets of sugarplums, gilded egg cups, and paper cornucopias filled with sweets and toys. From behind the tree, the grown-ups watched the children's faces as they opened the door and beheld this bright, sparkling miracle. The Follens' guest rightly prophesied "I have little doubt the Christmas tree will become one of the most flourishing exotics of New England."

In addition, many prepared salad dressings, imported olive oils, and imported vinegars (particularly balsamic) come in very intriguing bottles. I also pay attention to white wine bottles, especially those mildly tinted green. And many liqueur bottles have a potential second life as gift containers.

Two special little bottles, available in beautiful cobalt blue glass or translucent blue plastic, are made in France by Vallauris and found here in many gourmet food shops. I use one for the orange-flower water that goes in Brady Family Ginger Cookies (page 29) and another for the rose-flower water that is added to flavor crème anglaise. Another larger blue bottle is Crabtree & Evelyn's Almond Massage Oil.

In general, I pack colored liquids in colorless bottles and vice versa. Sometimes I add a drop or two of food coloring to an otherwise colorless, water-based liquid just for fun.

For nonliquid gifts there is of course the ever-useful basket. But I've found many other ways to deliver small treats. Large scallop shells, available in upscale kitchen stores, are perfect for small treats such as Chocolate Praline Truffles, Candied Peel, Bourbon Balls, and Glacé Nuts. For an equally grand effect, use a clear goblet. Straw paper plate liners hold cookies in style, especially if you line them with enormous painted gold leaves (see page 24). Keep an eye out for used odd china plates or mixing bowls, little mousse pots, terra-cotta flowerpots, and single cup-and-saucer combinations, and use these as containers.

Instead of using fragile shopping bags to deliver presents, I buy large brown cardboard storage boxes, spray them red or green, and stencil on a tree, a star, or the word "Noel".

HOW TO WRAP PROFESSIONALLY

Have you ever wondered why department store wrapping always has that "professional look"? Trying to match that style and neatness can be a frustrating experience.

When you measure your paper by eye, are you too miserly the first time around and too generous the second time? Does a straight edge elude you? Do your bows look, well, uh, rustic?

Oh, welcome, my friend. And hear the good news: You *can* learn the ways of the masters.

First of all, those department store wrapping wizards have a number of advantages that we mortals don't, such as standard-size boxes and paper cut to fit. They have ribbon on permanent rollers, tape in dispensers too heavy for anyone to borrow, scissors on leashes. They have a big, clean table that is never used for dinner or for sewing or for rolling out the pies. And yes, they do have experience, too.

But even if we can't match the facilities, I believe we *can* master the technique. Some time ago, I stopped by the wrapping department of a nearby department store and asked an expert for some advice. Here it is.

■ Have a good, clear space for wrapping, and use a table—*not* a bed.

■ Keep scissors, tape, pens, and ribbons within reach, and don't let anyone borrow them. If you are using rolls of paper, stand them up in an empty wastebasket. Slip a rubber band around each roll to keep it from unfurling.

■ Use as little tape as possible. (I use double-sided tape on the *inside* of the paper where it doesn't show.)

■ When wrapping a box, be sure to place it squarely in the middle of the paper. Keep the paper taut and the creases firm.

■ To wrap a cylinder, begin by cutting out two circles to cover the top and bottom. Wrap the rest of the cylinder, neatly folding paper over the top and bottom—then cover the folds on the ends with the cut-out circles. (Double-stick tape is especially effective here.)

■ To wrap a bottle, use reversible paper, such as tissue or mylar. Measure and cut the paper in a square that's twice the bottle height. Put the bottle in the middle of the square, draw up the corners, and tie a bow around the bottle neck. Pull out the corners of the square.

FOUR TIPS FOR WRAPPING PRESENTS

When it comes to wrapping presents, sometimes a little ingenuity can go a long way. Here are some of the little wrapping tricks I've used in years past.

■ *Look for "Christmas shoelaces"—red, green, and white—and use them instead of ribbon.*

■ *Tie a sprig of fresh rosemary under the bow. It will add a piny scent to your gifts.*

■ *Wrapping an oversized present? You can use a green trash bag, tied with a handsome, wide ribbon. I sometimes trim the top edge with pinking shears or stencil a design on the sides. If you want to completely disguise the bag, spray it lightly with gold.*

■ *Here's the perfect wrapping for a kitchen gift: Bundle it up in a brand-new dish towel, tied with yarn or ribbons. For the final flourish, embellish the top of your kitchen gift with a set of wooden spoons tied together with gold or red-and-green cord.*

GOLDEN LEAF GIFT WRAP

Yard after yard of wrapping paper beautifully decorated with the natural imprint of delicate leaves. It's easy to do—a great project for kids—and every sheet of homemade gold-leaf wrapping paper is as unique as a snowflake.

I begin collecting leaves in early fall and do my "printing" before they dry out. You can also use pressed, dried leaves. If it's too late in the season for green leaves, try this project using leaves from houseplants. Ivy is perfect. Use pressed, dried leaves or freshly picked leaves that are fairly flat (prominent veins make the most interesting print). You have the option of mixing different kinds of leaf patterns on the same paper or printing an entire sheet with one kind of leaf.

Wrapping paper? You have your choice. Bright, richly colored tissue paper is far and away the best, but you can also use brown wrapping paper or even recycle paper bags and newspaper.

This is a simple project that requires only a few supplies, including: gold acrylic paint from a tube or jar (*not* spray paint), a dish, newspaper, small paintbrush, and paper towels.

Squeeze paint into the dish. Holding a leaf by the stem, lay it flat on top of the newspaper. Paint one side, starting out with a heavy coat of gold paint.

Place the leaf, paint side down, on the wrapping paper. Use a paper towel to press the leaf gently against the wrapping paper. (Be careful not to move the leaf while pressing down.) Lift the leaf and repeat the print again without adding more paint. With each repetition, the imprint will become lighter and lighter. (Often, the veins of the leaves show up better with less paint.) For a brighter imprint, repaint the leaf and resume printing.

Variation: Use the same technique with small leaves to make matching gift tags. Stationery stores carry a variety of plain gift tags, or ask your stationer or printer for printers' stock samples. These usually come in a book or folder, and the paper is often very good quality. The size is perfect for gift tags.

Another alternative: Recycle last year's greeting cards by cutting the the unprinted stock into tag size.

To make a gold-leaf imprint, place a painted leaf on wrapping paper and press with a paper towel.

TIE THINGS UP WITH CURLYLOCKS

This is an easy, fluffy bow that you can make with paper curling ribbon. Children love to watch or help.

Cut an 8-yard length of ribbon. Curl the whole piece, using a blunt knife or scissors. Collect all the curls into a loose ball about 3 inches in diameter. Tie a small piece of ribbon around the middle to hold the ball together. If any "ringlets" are still loose, poke them into the center of the ball, using the eraser end of a pencil.

DECK THE HALLS

Boughs of holly are only the beginning. There are many sprigs, ribbons, and other signs of Christmas that make your home more festive—the "finishing touches" of the Christmas season.

■ Put a sprig of holly above every picture or mirror. Stick the sprig at a jaunty angle, stem down the back, between the picture and the wall.

■ Tie red ribbons above hanging plants. I leave the ends long, so they hang all the way down to the plants.

■ Stand gingerbread boys up against all your living room or dining room windows, as shown on page 134. (Not in the kitchen—your gingerbread boys will take a bow in all that moist heat.)

■ Hang wreaths on the inside of your windows, or even on an inside wall.

HOW TO TIE A FLORIST'S BOW

The basic florist's bow has two elements—the loops of ribbon that form the bow and the "streamers" from the center. Here are the steps for making a bow.

1. To determine the length of ribbon, decide how many loops you want in the bow and how long the streamers should be. For three 6-inch loops with two 1-foot streamers, use about 5 feet of ribbon. Cut into two pieces: one piece for the bow (3 feet) and one for the streamers (2 feet).

2. Cut two small pieces of florist's wire. Unless the ribbon you're using is very wide, 5-inch pieces of wire should be sufficient.

3. If the ribbon has a shiny side and a dull side, form the loops so the shiny side faces up. If both sides are the same, don't worry about which side is up.

4. Holding the loops between your thumb and forefinger, wrap the wire two or three times around the center to hold the loops of the bow. Then twist the wire behind the bow. (If using ribbon with a shiny side, twist the ribbon under the wire so the shiny side remains facing up.)

5. Wrap the streamer ribbon around the center of the bow and fasten in back with the second piece of florist's wire. Adjust the streamers, then tighten the wire.

THE CHRISTMAS MANTEL

I hope you have space on your mantel or the top of your buffet for your favorite reminders of the season. This is the place for treasures!

My mother festoons her mantel with greens, then tops it with little gingerbread boys. In our house, we have tall candles in brass candlesticks, with laurel garlands framing the tiny handmade crèche my mother-in-law brought back from France.

Among an assortment of greens, you can place a few red carnations with their stems in "orchid tubes"—containers shaped like small test tubes. (The stems, of course, are completely hidden by the greens.) And the greens form a perfect background for angels or elves.

WELCOMING LUMINARIA

The traditional Mexican luminaria (shown on page 126) is just a brown paper bag with a candle inside—a south-of-the-border "special effect" that has traveled well to New England. On Christmas Eve in many villages, luminaria line the way to church, Main Street, or the village green. The flickering glow of real candles works its own spell as carolers walk home along snowy paths.

To make luminaria Mexican-style, fill the bottoms of brown paper lunch bags with about 2 inches of sand. Fold the top of each bag *outward* and make a firm crease along the top of the fold: This will keep the mouth of the bag wide open. Set votive candles in the sand in the center of each bag, leaving the top wide open. When the candles are lit, flickering luminaria make a bright welcome along the front walk or driveway.

One of the best winter treats is a skating party. Call a few friends, bring along a tape player and some Strauss waltzes, and a Thermos of hot toddies (page 62). Then, skim across a pond ringed by luminaria.

BY THE LIGHT OF ORANGES

Hollowed-out oranges also make fragrant, glowing candle holders for votive candles. To make these unusual Christmas lights, cut off the top third of a large, thick-skinned orange. Before you scoop out the pulp, slice the skin into points like the top of a picket fence. Then scoop out the pulp, leaving as much clean pith as you can. Set a votive candle in the center of the orange and secure it with household glue.

I like to set these glowing orange candles on window sills—leaving the curtains open, of course. They're also a festive addition to any party table. As soon as you light them up, a nice orangy fragrance will begin to fill the room.

CHAPTER TEN

A CHRISTMAS STORY

a tale to tell by the fireside

There will never be a TV Christmas special to replace a real person reading a real story to a real listener. For one thing, TVs have no laps to sit on. Nor do they have arms to curl around you as you lean back and listen, waiting for each turn of the page to see a new picture, while a familiar voice fills your ears.

"How about a bedtime story?" are the words of comfort and safety and closeness that we've heard since childhood. No matter how grown-up we believe we are, a part of us, I think, still bends back to the gentle peace of story time, and especially to the closeness between reader and listener.

The first year we were married, when I was carrying Sarah and having trouble sleeping, Upton would read to me from Rudyard Kipling's *Just So Stories,* and I would drift right off, along the banks of "the great, gray-green, greasy Limpopo River, all set about with Fever trees." I can still hear the rise and fall of his voice, lapping like waves, soothing as a lullaby.

Christmas is the best time of all for reading aloud, and the story that follows is perfect for the season. *The Very Best Christmas Tree*, written by Tony King, with wood engravings by Michael McCurdy, is certainly one that children will enjoy. And it's an appropriate choice if you, like the Bones family in the story, set up your card table in the kitchen after Thanksgiving and "take turns making decorations before breakfast, dinner, and bedtime."

THE VERY BEST
CHRISTMAS TREE

The Bones Family lived in a funny old house with a front hall that looked as if it had been designed with a big Christmas tree in mind.

When the children were small, Mr. Bones started bringing the Christmas tree home as a surprise. On the first snowy day in December, he would drive to the Southwick Farm in Leicester, Massachusetts, and climb into the battered truck with Farmer Southwick. With the Southwicks' old dog running alongside, they would drive out the farm road behind the barn, through the ravine by the pond, past the woods where the laurel grows, and up to the high meadow where the tallest evergreens stand.

Each year as they tied the tree to the roof of Mr. Bones's car, Farmer Southwick said, "Be careful you don't bust a gut."

The Boneses decorated their tree almost entirely with ornaments they made themselves. After Thanksgiving, a card table was set up in the kitchen so the whole family could take turns making decorations before breakfast, dinner, and bedtime.

Every year there were more and more beautiful handmade ornaments, which gave Mr. Bones an excuse to buy a bigger tree than they'd had the year before.

At last the tree was so large that guests had to enter the house through the back door. To climb the front stairs, they had to hug the wall. The little girl whose bedroom was on the third floor could see the top of the tree without getting out of bed.

Each year after the tree was decorated, Mr. Bones would exclaim, "This is definitely the most beautiful tree we've ever had!" And everyone would agree.

One Christmas Mr. Bones noticed that Mrs. Bones was very quiet. He asked if something was wrong. She looked a bit sad and said she wished their friends didn't have to come into the house through the kitchen, and that she was afraid of what might happen

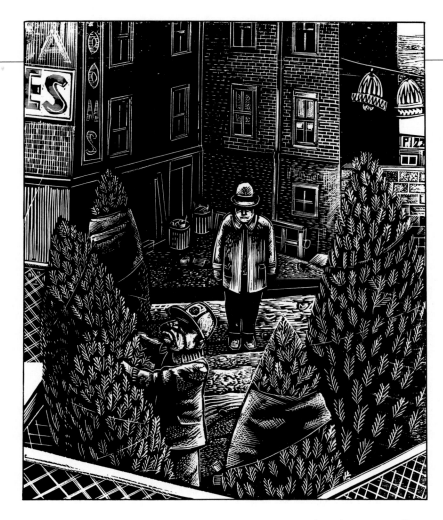

if such a big tree caught fire. Mr. Bones promised to buy a smaller tree next year.

But when the time came, the tree he bought was almost as big as the last one. He explained that it had looked smaller before they cut it down. When Mrs. Bones saw it, she sat on the bottom stair and cried. This made Mr. Bones feel like crying too. He promised she could have any tree she liked next Christmas.

Early next December, Mrs. Bones called Mr. Bones at work and asked him to pick up a tree she had chosen. The tree cost twice as much as one of Mr. Southwick's, and the sales attendant smelled of stale beer. The snow around the edge of the vacant city lot looked grimy, and Mr. Bones thought of Mr. Southwick's old dog running beside the truck through the clean snow. When he tied the tree to the car, there was certainly no need for anyone to warn him about busting a gut.

Mrs. Bones's tree was small enough so that it could be set up in the middle of the front hall. It looked lovely, in its own way. Fat and even all around. But it couldn't hold all the homemade decorations and was only big enough for one string of colorful wooden beads. And because the tree had been cut early for its long trip to the city, many of its needles had fallen by Christmas Day.

The children told Mr. Bones when no one else could hear that they liked Mummy's tree okay, but they hoped he would be the one to pick out the tree next Christmas.

Mr. Bones had a better idea. That very day he made a date with Mrs. Bones to go to the Southwick Farm on the first day it snowed the following December to pick out the tree together.

And that is what happened. On the first snowy day in December, Mr. and Mrs. Bones visited Farmer Southwick. They climbed in the truck and drove out the farm road behind the barn, through the ravine by the pond, past the woods where the laurel grows, and up to the high meadow where the tallest evergreens stand, while the old dog ran alongside through the fresh snow.

They picked out a tree, perhaps smaller than Mr. Bones would have preferred and perhaps larger than the one Mrs. Bones would have chosen, but it was a beautiful tree. The children cheered when they saw it. The tree held all the beloved ornaments and all three strings of colorful wooden beads, and friends could still squeeze in by the front door.

Although the little girl whose bedroom was on the third floor couldn't see the tree without getting out of bed, she could smell it first thing in the morning when she woke because it was so freshly cut.

Everyone agreed it was the most beautiful tree they had ever had.

By Tony King
Illustrated by Michael McCurdy

PHOTO CREDITS

INDEX

NOTE: Page references in *italic* indicate photographs and illustrations.